ENDURANCE RUNNING EVENTS
by Norman Brook

Previous publications in this series:

Middle Distance Running and Steeplechasing (J.W.Ll. Alford) 1951
Reprinted 1955
Second Edition 1960
Third Edition 1965
Middle Distance Running (A.P. Ward) 1967
Reprinted 1972
Middle and Long Distance, Marathon and Steeplechase
   (D.C.V. Watts & H. Wilson) 1976
This Edition under new title 1992
Reprinted 1998

ISBN   0 85134 106 3   1K/4K/46K/07.98

ABOUT THE AUTHOR

Norman D. Brook was appointed National Athletics Coach to Northern Ireland in 1982 and Chief Coach for Endurance Events in 1985. He was born and educated in Scotland where he also taught in a secondary school. In 1978 he returned to higher education to study Coaching Science at Dunfermline College of Physical Education (Edinburgh) and at Lakehead University (Canada).

Norman has been a coach to several Great Britain international athletes and has been a team coach at the Olympic Games, European Championships, World Student Games and Commonwealth Games.

ACKNOWLEDGMENTS

The author extends his thanks to the following people:

— to Claire, for her support and encouragement
— to Gordon Surtees and Harry Harvey for their advice in the writing of this book
— to the many coaches, athletes and physiologists that have contributed to his understanding of the theory and practice of endurance running
— to Frank W. Dick for his advice and especially for his patience
— to Stan Greenberg for his help with the historical section
— to Claire Brook, Ursula McKee, Niamh Murphy, Mark Kirk and Brian Treacy for their assistance in the photographs
— to Gerry Fitzgerald for his photographs and Howard Payne for providing photo sequences

Dedicated to all those involved in athletics in Northern Ireland who project the positive side of life in the province so well and provide the opportunity for young people to work together.

CONTENTS

CHAPTER 1
INTRODUCTION

The term "endurance events" in track and field athletics refers to those events which take place over distances from 800m upwards. Running events include those which take place on the track ranging from the 800m to the 10,000m, road races including the marathon, cross country races and specialist events such as fell running and ultra long distance running. This book limits itself to those endurance running events conducted at major championships such as the Olympic Games and the European and World Championships. However, readers with a special interest in events such as cross country running or road racing will find that the training principles outlined in this book can be applied to their area of interest.

All endurance running events require an ability to judge pace and distribute effort over the distance to be covered. They also require competitors to cope with running in a group and to deal with those tactical considerations which arise as a consequence of the runners not being restricted to individual lanes. Despite these commonalities, the duration and speed at which each of the endurance running events is run place varying individual demands on the competitor. These demands need to be considered and prepared for if the endurance runner is to be successful in competition.

This book concentrates on preparation for those endurance events which are currently contested in major championships: the 800m, 1500m, 3000m (women), 5000m (men), 10,000m, marathon and 3000m steeplechase (men).

Over the last two decades or so women's endurance competition has moved towards equal standing with the men at championships. They do not currently compete in the steeplechase, although it is envisaged that such an event will be introduced at some future date, and it is expected that eventually the 3000m will be replaced by the 5000m.

THE ENDURANCE RUNNING EVENTS
800 Metres
The 800m race consists of two laps of a standard 400m track. As with all endurance races, the race is started by the command "on your marks", calling the athletes to the start line, followed by the firing of a gun to signal the start. The first bend of the 800m race is run in lanes, until the runners pass a curved green line which is located at the point where the bend unwinds into the back straight. After passing this point the runners can break lanes and run to the inside of the track (see Figure 1).

In club or school races where there are more competitors than lanes, it is possible to start from a curved start line, breaking for the inside of the track from the start. For safety it is recommended that on six lane tracks no more than 10 runners start from a curved line, and for eight lane tracks no more than 12.

The 800m is often described as an extended sprint event. It attracts athletes from both speed (former sprinters who have moved up distance) and endurance backgrounds (middle and long distance runners moving down distance).

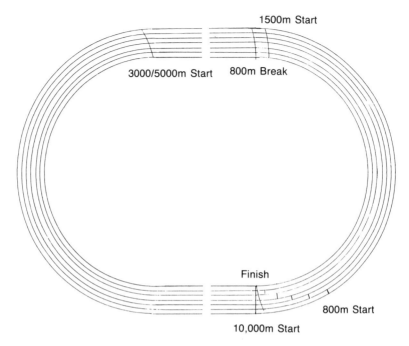

Fig. 1 Start, break and finish lines for endurance track events.

1500 Metres

The 1500m race starts from a curved line positioned at the start of the back straight. The runners break for the inside of the track from the start and run three and three quarter laps of the track (see Figure 1).

Being the metric equivalent of the mile, this event is considered by many to be the "Blue Riband" of track and field athletics. It is usually one of the last events to be held in a championships, providing a climax to the competition.

3000 Metres

This race is a women's event in major championships, but it is also a popular distance for men at non-championship meetings. It starts at the 200m start and features seven-and-a-half laps of the track (see Figure 1).

5000 Metres

Currently a men's event in major championships, it starts from the same line as the 3000m and features twelve-and-a-half laps of the track.

10,000 Metres

The longest running event conducted on the track at championships, it starts at the start/finish line and consists of 25 laps of the track. It is also a popular distance for road races.

Marathon

The longest championship running event, the marathon usually starts and finishes in the main stadium with most of the distance of 26 miles and 385 yards (42.195 kilometres) being covered on the road. The event was created in 1896 on the occasion of the first modern Olympics. A Greek Olympic delegate offered Baron Pierre de Coubertin a trophy to commemorate the epic run of the Greek soldier Pheidippides from Marathon to Athens. Legend has it that in 490BC the soldier ran between the two cities, which were actually 35 kilometres apart, bearing news of the Greeks' victory over the Persians. When he arrived in Athens, he imparted the news, collapsed and died.

Between 1896 and 1908, the marathon was held over varying distances. The plan for the 1908 Games which were held in London was that the race would be held over 26 miles, running from the start outside Windsor Castle and finishing in the White City Stadium. In order that the royal family could view the start, the organisers were then obliged late in the day to start the race outside the windows of the castle. The race also had to finish opposite the royal box in the stadium. This could only be achieved by adding 385 yards on to the planned 26 miles. In 1924 the distance of the 1908 race was taken as the standard distance and the marathon has been this unusual length since this date.

3000m Steeplechase

The position of the start and the number of laps to be run in the 3000m steeplechase vary according to the position of the water jump, which can be located either inside or outside the track. This has the effect of lengthening or shortening each lap of the track. If the water jump is on the inside of the track each lap is shortened by approximately 10 metres, and the start will be

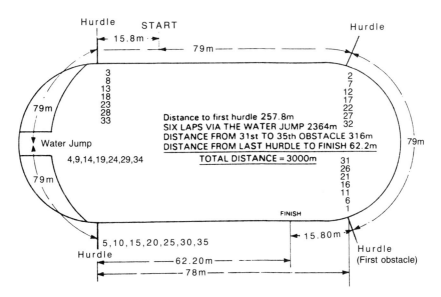

Fig. 2 Positions of water jump and barriers for 3000m steeplechase event.

3

on the back straight about 270m from the finish line. The start of the race on a track where the water jump is located on the outside will be on the home straight, about 130m from the finish line, and each lap will be approximately 410 metres in length.

In the 3000m steeplechase there are 28 hurdles and 7 water jumps to be negotiated. The first hurdle is placed at least 10 metres from the finish line, the second hurdle about the start of the back straight, the third before the end of the back straight and the fourth in the home straight at least 68m back from the finish line (see Figure 2). Competitors in the 3000m steeplechase should not meet any hurdles until after they enter the first full lap, the hurdles being removed until after they have run to the start of their first lap.

A steeplechase hurdle is 0.914 metres high (3ft) and is at least 3.96 metres wide (13ft). Usually the first hurdle is extended to at least 5.00m to allow for the runners being closely bunched at this early stage of the race. The top of the hurdle is 127mm (5in) square and, when set on the track, one end should project 0.30 metres over the inside edge of the track. Steeplechase hurdles should weigh between 80kg and 100kg and are designed so that they will not topple over.

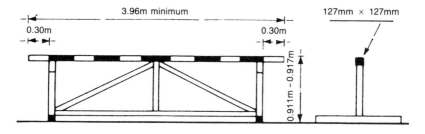

Fig. 3 A steeplechase barrier.

The water jump hurdle is a similar height, but is only 3.66m wide. The water jump is 3.66 metres × 3.66 metres and it should be filled so that the water is level with the track surface. At the barrier end the water will be 70cm deep for 30cm and it then slopes up to the track. The synthetic track surface should be laid about 2.5 metres into the water in order to ensure a safe landing.

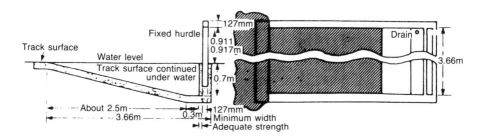

Fig. 4 A steeplechase water jump barrier.

The long run to the first hurdle allows the runners to break from the curved starting line for the inside of the track and to take up their preferred positions before encountering the first barrier.

As steeplechasers tend to get wet when negotiating the water jump, they need to take care in selecting their shorts and vests to ensure that they do not become transparent when wet.

PREPARATION FOR SUCCESS

The aim of this book is to examine those factors which contribute to preparation for successful participation in the seven running events identified. Preparation to compete in endurance events requires consideration of those factors which influence performance. Having done this, strategies can then be developed to prepare runners to meet the demands of the event the runner wishes to compete in and the demands of the annual competition programme.

There is a need to consider those factors which determine performance and to identify training and other strategies which will effect an improvement in those factors. The main factors which influence performance in an endurance running event are as follows:

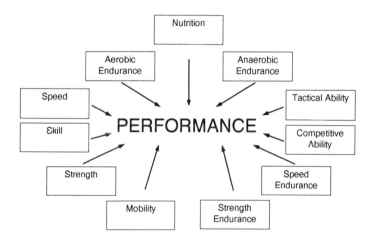

Figure 5: *Performance factors in endurance running*

Improvements in these factors will lead to improved performance in endurance events:

Aerobic Endurance
— improving the contribution this energy system can make to the total energy demands of the event.
— holding back recruitment of the anaerobic energy system which produces lactic acid.
— allowing the runner to recover quickly in training, enabling a high quality of training to be maintained.
— improving the marathon runner's utilisation of fats as an energy source.

Anaerobic Endurance
— improving the contribution this system can make to the energy demands of the event as evidenced by an increased peak lactic acid level.
— improving the runner's ability to tolerate high levels of lactic acid.

Strength Endurance
— allowing the runner to resist fatigue and to continue to express strength despite the presence of high lactic acid concentrations.

Speed Endurance
— allowing the runner to resist fatigue and maintain speed over the duration of the race.
— allowing the runner to cope with the demands of changes of pace during the course of the race.
— allowing the runner to accelerate (kick) and produce a fast sprint finish in the closing stages of a race despite the fatigue caused by increased anaerobic energy production.

Speed
— allowing the competitive distance to be run at a fast pace.
— allowing the runner to accelerate (kick) and produce a fast sprint finish in the closing stages of a race.

Mobility
— allowing sufficient ranges of movement to enable sprinting and hurdling techniques to be developed.
— enabling the runner to avoid injury.

Strength
— contributing to the development of running speed.
— protecting weak areas of the body which are susceptible to injury.

Skill
— enabling an economical running action and ability to sprint as required.
— enabling an efficient hurdling technique and water jump clearance.

Tactical Ability
— developing the ability to analyse the competitive situation, to make decisions and take actions which will increase the likelihood of a successful outcome.

Competitive Ability
— developing the ability to produce the best possible personal effort, even in situations where the probability of success is low and the task difficulty high.

Nutrition
— ensuring the ample supply of nutrients which provide energy and maintain the body's function.

These various factors will be brought together through careful planning of training, competition and support services. The importance of each factor will vary depending on the runner's main event, age, sex, previous experience and standard. These are taken into consideration in the following chapters.

STANDARDS OF PERFORMANCE

There are a large number of individuals participating seriously in endurance running events. Serious participation is considered to take place when an individual prepares for competition by undertaking training on a regular basis, regardless of the individual's standard and the number of training sessions undertaken each week. The following performance standards are offered as a guide to the runner's level of performance.

Classification Criteria
(Approximate to standard at given levels in an average year)

1)	Under 15 National	— Top 30 UK
2)	Under 15 Elite	— Top 10 UK
3)	Under 17 National	— Top 30 UK
4)	Under 17 Elite	— Top 10 UK
5)	Under 20 National	— Top 30 UK
6)	Under 20 Elite	— Top 10 UK
7)	Under 20 International	— Top 10 World
8)	Senior National	— Top 50 UK
9)	Senior Elite	— Top 10 UK
10)	Senior International	— Top 30 World

(See Table 1 on next page)

EVENT	Under 15 National	Under 15 Elite	Under 17 National	Under 17 Elite	Under 20 National	Under 20 Elite	Under 20 International	Senior National	Senior Elite	Senior International
800m Men	2.07:00	2.03:00	1.58:00	1.56:00	1.53:50	1.52:00	1.48:00	1.50:00	1.47:00	1.45:00
800m Women	2.20:00	2.17:00	2.17:00	2.14:00	2.15:00	210:00	2.03:50	2.09:00	2.04:00	1.59:00
1500m Men	4.25:00	4.18:00	4.05:00	4.00:00	3.55:00	3.51:00	3.43:00	3.46:00	3.39:00	3.36:00
1500m Women	5.00:00	4.45:00	4.45:00	4.40:00	4.40:00	4.26:00	4.16:00	4.25:00	4.10:00	4.06:00
3000m Men	9.45:00	9.37:00	9.00:00	8.45:00	8.40:00	8.23:00	8.13:00	8.05:00	7.55:00	7.48:00
3000m Women			10.40:00	10.10:00	10.00:00	9.50:00	9.08:50	9.40.00	9.05:00	8.47:50
5000m Men					15.30:00	14.56:00	14.05:00	14.05:00	13.35:00	13.24:00
10,000m Men							29.20:00	30.00:00	28.25:00	27.57:00
10,000m Women								37.30:00	34.20.00	32.10:00
Steeple-chase			4.40:00	4.28:00	9.45:00	9.30:00	8.52:00	9.10:00	8.42:00	8.23:00
Marathon Men								2.23:00	2.16:00	2.11:00
Marathon Women								2.57:00	2.43:00	2.30:30

Table 1: *Performance standards in endurance running*

CHAPTER 2

DEVELOPING ENDURANCE

Two energy systems contribute significant amounts of energy for endurance running activity, the aerobic system and the lactic anaerobic system. The purpose of endurance training is to develop these two systems. Both systems contribute to the energy demands of each of the endurance running events to a greater or lesser extent. Their importance to success in each event will be reflected in the mix of aerobic and anaerobic endurance work included as general or specific training.

General endurance training is aimed at developing a level of aerobic and anaerobic endurance which will allow the runner to accept and benefit from specific training. General endurance training always precedes specific endurance training.

Specific endurance training prepares the runner to meet the demands of his chosen event. This type of training is essential to improved performance but it can only be employed successfully if the runner has developed a solid foundation of general endurance.

DEVELOPING GENERAL ENDURANCE

Aerobic Endurance

All runners competing in endurance based events need to develop high levels of aerobic endurance regardless of their competitive distance. The aerobic system contributes a higher proportion of the energy requirements in longer running events such as the marathon in comparison to shorter events such as the 800m. This does not however mean that it is more important to develop aerobic fitness in long distance events that in the middle distance events. The development of aerobic endurance as a general endurance factor is equally important in all of the endurance running events and it is undoubtedly a key factor to success in all of these events.

Training to develop a runner's general aerobic endurance serves two main functions:

— it increases the amount of energy that can be made available through aerobic metabolism holding back recruitment of the anaerobic energy system with its by-product of lactic acid.

— it improves the runner's rate of recovery allowing improved quality of training in mixed or anaerobic training sessions.

Aerobic Training Methods

Aerobic endurance for running is best developed through three types of running activity:

1. Continuous Running — Steady State.
2. Continuous Running — Mixed Intensity.
3. Intermittent Running.

Continuous Running — Steady State

Continuous running forms the background to most endurance based runners'

9

training programmes. Distances run vary from short runs of 2-3 miles to long runs which may exceed 20 miles. The effort expended during these runs is related to their duration. Effort can be expressed as running speed, heart rate or as a percentage of the runner's maximum aerobic power. The terms short, medium and long runs will have different meanings to athletes in different endurance events. The 800m runner might consider six miles to be a long run, whilst to a marathon runner a long run might mean something in excess of 15 miles.

Long Slow Run	—	Ovett/Coe	—	12 miles
	—	Moorcroft	—	15 miles
Medium Run	—	Ovett	—	5-8 miles
	—	Coe	—	6-9 miles
	—	Moorcroft	—	8-12 miles

A common feature of this type of running is that the effort remains constant throughout the duration of the run. This means that running speed, heart rate and the percentage of maximal aerobic power remain fairly constant, producing what we call a steady state.

Steady state continuous runs are generally classified as long, medium or short duration runs.

1. *Long Duration Runs*
   - Duration of at least 45 mins, often more.
   - Distances greater than 10 miles can extend up to 20 miles and more for runners preparing for the marathon.
   - Effort during runs corresponds to a heart rate of 130-160 bpm or a percentage maximal aerobic power of 60-75%.

2. *Medium Duration Runs*
   - Duration of 30-45 mins.
   - Distances of 4-8 miles.
   - Effort during runs corresponds to a heart rate of 150-170 bpm or a percentage maximal aerobic power of 75-85%.

3. *Short Duration Runs*
   - Duration of up to 30 mins.
   - Distances of 3-5 miles.
   - Effort during runs corresponds to a heart rate of 160-180 bpm or a percentage maximal aerobic power of 85-90%.

When on a continuous run, the runner will quickly settle into a pace which is appropriate to the distance being covered. Having achieved a steady state, heart rate and maximum aerobic power remain relatively steady, rising only if the pace is increased or the terrain becomes difficult, e.g. running uphill. Short duration runs are completed at a higher intensity than long or medium duration runs. The effort required is such that the runner needs to concentrate for the duration and the term sustained run is often used as a description.

Continuous Runs — Varied Pace

An alternative to running a set course at the same pace is to vary your speed during the course of a run. This type of training was introduced by Gosta Holmer, the Swedish National Coach during the early 1940s. The term he used for this type of training was 'fartlek' which in Swedish means "speed-play". During Holmer's continuous runs the natural terrain of the Swedish woods was used to vary the running speed.

Such training not only stimulates aerobic development but also encourages speed itself, the ability to change speed and a certain degree of mental resilience.

Varied pace continuous runs can be organised in two ways:

1. *Fartlek*

Based on Holmer's original concept, the athlete sets out on a run in the woods or over a country course. During the run the athlete changes pace according to how he feels or as is appropriate to the natural terrain. The ideal is to use the natural terrain to test yourself, i.e. when you reach a hill you work hard up the hill, on a downhill section you lower the pace to recover, then on a flat stretch you perform a series of sprints. Good fartlek trainers are able to work hard throughout their training runs (see Figure 6).

1 Fast Pace over Flat Ground
2 Steady Recovery Pace Downhill
3 Fast Pace over Short Flat Section
4 Sprint Up Hill Section
5 Steady Recovery Pace on Flat Section
6 Sprint Up Stepped Section
Vary Route - Efforts Respond to Nature of Terrain

Fig. 6 Fartlek running.

2. *Varied Pace Runs*

A more formal approach to varied pace running is to set parameters prior to the start of a run. A coach for example might ask his runners to run a 4 mile fartlek dividing the run into 8 half mile sections and varying the pace for each section (see also Figure 7, based on a 3000m course).

3000m Course

1 800m Fast Pace
2 400m Steady/Recovery Pace
3 1000m Steady Pace
4 400m Fast Pace
5 400m Steady/Recovery Pace
Repeat Circuit - Distances of Efforts Pre-Determined

Fig. 7 Varied pace running.

Intermittent Running

The third form of aerobic training is intermittent running, where the running session is broken into a series of runs interspersed with rest periods. This allows the total distance being run to be completed at much faster speeds. Increasing the intensity of the runs requires a higher working heart rate and greater percentage of maximal aerobic power to be tapped.

An example of this would be undertaking four 1 mile runs with a rest in between each run of 2 mins. The total time taken for the four runs would be much faster than the time that could be achieved on a 4 mile continuous run.

Intermittent runs are more commonly known in running circles as interval or repetition runs. The term interval running is most commonly used in con-

12

nection with training aimed at developing aerobic endurance. There are two main types of intermittent or interval running for aerobic endurance:

1. *Long Aerobic Intervals*
   - Runs of 2-8 mins duration
   - Heart rate of 180-190 bpm and 90-100% Vo2 Max
   - Short recovery 1-4 mins
   - Heart rate should fall to about 120-130 bpm during recovery.

   Example: 5 × 1000m with easy 200m jog recovery.

2. *Short Aerobic Intervals*
   - Runs of 100-400m @ 75% of best time for distance
   - Heart rate of 180 bpm and 90-100% Vo2 Max
   - Short recovery of 30 secs-2 mins
   - Heart rate should fall to about 120-130 bpm during recovery.

   Example: 12 × 300m with a 100m jog recovery.

Progressing Aerobic Training

Training to develop aerobic endurance should be progressed gradually over a number of weeks (see Chapter 5). Steady state continuous runs can be gradually increased in distance. Once the maximum distance required has been established, the time taken to complete the distance can be improved. Varied pace runs such as fartlek training can also be gradually increased in duration. Once the maximum distance has been achieved the quality of these runs can be developed.

Interval training to develop aerobic endurance can be advanced by slowly progressing through the following stages:

A. Increase the number of repetitions.
B. Increase the distance of repetitions.
C. Decrease the recovery period.
D. Increase the speed of repetitions.

Example:

8 × 200m in 32 secs with 2 mins recovery.
A
12 × 200m in 32 secs with 2 mins recovery.
B
10 × 300m in 50 secs with 2 mins recovery.
C
10 × 300m in 50 secs with 60 secs recovery.
D
10 × 300m in 48 secs with 60 secs recovery.

Monitoring Heart Rate

Both the intensity of training and recovery rates can be monitored using the heart rate. Suggested heart rates were given in the previous descriptions of aerobic training methods as a guide to the intensity of effort required.

The heart rate can be monitored during both continuous and intermittent runs using a pulse meter (see Figure 8). These are relatively inexpensive and have the advantage of giving the runner continuous feedback. Some pulse meters will record the pulse over time, allowing a graph to be produced of heart rate during the session.

Fig. 8

The coach can also monitor heart rate at the beginning and end of runs using a stopwatch and the chart detailed below if he does not have access to a pulse meter. The pulse is located behind the athlete's thumb on the radial (wrist) artery or at the neck on the carotid artery. The middle and index fingers should be used to find the pulse and not the thumb as it has its own pulse. If the runner is counting his own heart beats, he can as an alternative place his hand over his chest. The heart beat/pulse is easier to locate after the athlete has been running. A count of 10 beats is timed, starting the watch on a beat and then stopping the watch on the tenth following beat. The time recorded is found on the chart to indicate the heart rate.

This method has the advantage for coaches of quickly assessing heart rate after a run before it starts to fall. Well conditioned runners recover quickly which is evidenced by a rapid return of the heart rate to about 120-130 bpm.

Time	Rate	Time	Rate
3.0	200	6.6	91
3.1	194	6.7	90
3.2	188	6.8	88
3.3	182	6.9	87
3.4	176	7.0	86
3.5	171	7.1	85
3.6	167	7.2	83
3.7	162	7.3	82
3.8	158	7.4	81
3.9	154	7.5	80
4.0	150	7.6	79
4.1	146	7.7	78
4.2	143	7.8	77
4.3	139	7.9	76
4.4	136	8.0	75
4.5	133	8.1	74
4.6	130	8.2	73
4.7	128	8.3	72
4.8	125	8.4	71
4.9	122	8.5	70.5
5.0	120	8.6	70
5.1	118	8.7	69
5.2	115	8.8	68
5.3	113	8.9	67
5.4	111	9.0	66.5
5.5	109	9.1	66
5.6	107	9.2	65
5.7	105	9.3	64.5
5.8	103	9.4	64
5.9	102	9.5	63
6.0	100	9.6	62.5
6.1	98	9.7	62
6.2	97	9.8	61
6.3	95	9.9	60.5
6.4	94	10.0	60
6.5	92		

Table 2: *Heart rate chart.*

ANAEROBIC ENDURANCE

Strength Endurance

The need to develop anaerobic endurance varies according to the distance being run. Generally the longer the competitive distance, the less this system contributes to the energy demands of the event. There is however a case for all runners developing basic levels of general anaerobic conditioning in the muscles involved in the running action. These should involve muscle groups which play both a supportive and a propulsive role. Developing the ability of these muscle groups to perform work despite a build up of lactic acid, improves the runner's ability to accept and benefit from specific training and to withstand fatigue in the competitive situation. This type of anaerobic work is closely related to the strength of the muscles and is known as strength endurance.

Strength endurance training requires overcoming a load in the presence of lactic acid. Some aspects of this type of training are closely related to strength training where muscle groups are isolated in specific exercises. If high repetitions and short recoveries are used an anaerobic training effect will be produced. Other activities which involve running with a resistance will also develop strength endurance. These include hill running, sand dune running, resistance running, repetitions with a very short recovery and strength endurance drills. The use of exercises involving either bodyweight or some additional weight in the form of circuit or stage training is described in Chapter 3. The use of running with additional loadings or reduced recoveries is described here.

1. *Hill Runs*

   Hills are often used as part of a continuous run to help develop aerobic endurance by making the runner work at higher heart rates than could be achieved at similar running speeds on a flat course. However, to give the maximum benefit as an anaerobic training method the runner will need to sprint up the hill. Training is organised in sets and repetitions such as 2 sets of 6 repetitions of a 150-200m hill with a jog back down the hill recovery. Distances will vary according to the incline of the hill and the speed of running. Care should be taken not to use too steep a hill as this will interfere with the running action which should reflect good sprinting form.

2. *Sand Dune Running*

   Sand dune running is again organised in sets and repetitions such as 2 sets of 6 repetitions with a jog back down recovery. Distances to be run will be much shorter than those used for hills as the sand tends to give way and to make it much harder to run up. This is a good type of early preparation training, but it should be avoided later in the training programme as it does not encourage good running technique or speed.

3. *Resistance Running*

   Resistance running consists of fast running or sprinting with an additional load such as pulling a drag. Such training may be useful for 800m runners but is of questionable value to runners training for longer distances (see Figure 57 on page 37).

4. *Repetition runs with insufficient recovery times*

   Fast runs with such short recoveries that they do not allow the runner to recover fully build up high levels of lactic acid. This type of work does not allow the athlete to maintain quality so it cannot be considered as specific training. It does build up high levels of lactic acid though, and may be useful in developing the lactic buffers.

   Examples:
   a) Back to Back 100m with 20-30 secs recovery.
      6-8 repetitions per set, 2-3 sets.

b) **20 Second Runs.**
Run flat out and mark how far you run in 20 seconds. Take 15 mins rest. Start a set of runs with 90 seconds recovery to try and run within 10 metres of your mark. Stop when you have two consecutive failures. Repeat for a second set.

5. *Strength Endurance Drills*
Drills such as high knee lifts and recovery leg action illustrated in Chapter 4 can be used as strength endurance drills. This is achieved by asking the runner to perform the drill at normal speed but to keep repeating the action until lactic acid starts to build up in the legs. Performing these drills for 45-60 seconds or over 100m are examples.

SPECIFIC ENDURANCE

Runners need to develop endurance which allows them to meet the energy demands of their event. Each of the endurance events places its own unique mix of aerobic and anaerobic energy demands on the individual runner. In aiming to meet these specific energy demands, training is organised to replicate the stress of the event in order to stimulate the body to adapt to those demands. This however is only done after the runner has established a sound base of general aerobic endurance.

Training to develop specific endurance is aimed at allowing the runner to sustain a fast pace over the duration of the race. The training is therefore closely related to the runner's racing speed. By organising training at speeds close to racing speed, the specific combinations of the aerobic and anaerobic energy systems can be recruited.

The effect of such training is to cause adaptations at a muscular level. As muscle fibre recruitment is specific to the speed at which the athlete runs, a training effect can only be beneficial if the training is at speeds close to racing pace. The adaptations which take place at a muscular level will be both aerobic and anaerobic. In events like the 800m, 1500m, 3000m and 3000m steeplechase, the pace at which they are run will place high energy demands on the muscles, requiring them to produce a high amount of energy anaerobically. In such events this ability to produce and tolerate high levels of lactate is a contributing factor to success. As the distance being run increases through the long distances towards the marathon, the importance of the anaerobic energy system diminishes.

Specific Training — Track Events

Training to develop specific endurance for track events takes the form of intermittent training and is often referred to as interval or repetition running. As it is impossible to replicate racing conditions constantly in training, training to develop specific endurance has to involve repetitions shorter than racing distance, being run at or faster than race pace, interspersed with recovery periods. Training to develop the ability to sustain race pace is often pursued by two types of repetition running:

1. *Short Repetitions with Short Recoveries*
   - Distances of 200m-2000m (distances depend on event)
   - Run at race pace or faster
   - Short recoveries ½-2 × work effort

- Training organised in sets
- Longer recovery between sets.

Examples:

Event	No. of Sets	No. of Reps	Distance	Recovery	Rest
800m	2-3	4	200m	30 secs	10 mins +
1500m	2	3	500m	45 secs	10 mins +
3000m	1-2	5	600m	200m	10 mins +
5000m	1-2	5	1000m	200m	10 mins +
10,000m	2	5	1000m	200m	10 mins +

2. *Long Repetitions with Long Recoveries*
- Distances of 600m-5000m
- Run at close to racing pace
- Long recoveries of 10-20 mins
- A few runs only.

Examples:

Event	No. of Reps	Distance	Recovery
800m	3	600m	15-20 mins
1500m	2-3	1000m	15-20 mins
3000m	2	1500m	15-20 mins
5000m		3000m	5-10 mins
		2000m	
		1000m	
10,000m		4000m	5-10 mins
		3000m	
		2000m	
		1000m	

Race pace referred to above is the pace for the athlete's competitive distance and not the training distance. The runs detailed above would be run at or faster than race pace. Table 3 is a useful guide to racing pace.

Mixed Pace Training

Of course not all races are conducted at a steady pace and this needs to be considered when planning specific training. A race may start at a faster pace and then slow down, or it may start at a slow pace and then gradually wind up to a faster pace. The pace may change in the middle of the race, either by a runner inserting a series of surges or by him throwing in a fast lap. Such variations in pace need to be prepared for in training.

This can be achieved by varying speeds of different units of training on different days. A 1500m runner, for example, might train at 400m, 800m, 1500m and 3000m paces. This might be arranged by training at different paces on different days.

Examples:

Day 1: 3 × 1000m @ 1500m pace.
Day 2: 5 ×   300m @   400m pace.

AVG. PER 200/400m (SECS.)	600	800	1000	1500	2000	3000	4000	5000	6000	8000	10,000
25.0/50.0	1:15.0	1:40.0	—	—	—	—	—	—	—	—	—
25.5/51.0	1:16.5	1:42.0	—	—	—	—	—	—	—	—	—
26.0/52.0	1:18.0	1:44.0	2:10.0	—	—	—	—	—	—	—	—
26.5/53.0	1:19.5	1:46.0	2:12.5	—	—	—	—	—	—	—	—
27.0/54.0	1:21.0	1:48.0	2:15.0	—	—	—	—	—	—	—	—
27.5/55.0	1:22.5	1:50.0	2:17.5	—	—	—	—	—	—	—	—
28.0/56.0	1:24.0	1:52.0	2:20.0	3:30.0	—	—	—	—	—	—	—
28.5/57.0	1:25.5	1:54.0	2:22.5	3:33.8	—	—	—	—	—	—	—
29.0/58.0	1:27.0	1:56.0	2:25.0	3:37.5	4:50.0	—	—	—	—	—	—
29.5/59.0	1:28.5	1:58.0	2:27.5	3:41.3	4:55.0	—	—	—	—	—	—
30.0/60.0	1:30.0	2:00.0	2:30.0	3:45.0	5:00.0	7:30.0	—	—	—	—	—
30.5/61.0	1:31.5	2:02.0	2:32.5	3:48.8	5:05.0	7:37.5	10:10.0	—	—	—	—
31.0/62.0	1:33.0	2:04.0	2:35.0	3:52.5	5:10.0	7:45.0	10:20.0	12:55.0	—	—	—
31.5/63.0	1:34.5	2:06.0	2:37.5	3:56.3	5:15.0	7:52.5	10:30.0	13:07.5	15:45.0	—	—
32.0/64.0	1:36.0	2:08.0	2:40.0	4:00.0	5:20.0	8:00.0	10:40.0	13:20.0	16:00.0	21:20.0	—
32.5/65.0	1:37.5	2:10.0	2:42.5	4:03.8	5:25.0	8:07.5	10:50.0	13:32.5	16:15.0	21:40.0	27:05.0
33.0/66.0	1:39.0	2:12.0	2:45.0	4:07.5	5:30.0	8:15.0	11:00.0	13:45.0	16:30.0	22:00.0	27:30.0
33.5/67.0	1:40.5	2:14.0	2:47.5	4:11.3	5:35.0	8:22.5	11:10.0	13:57.5	16:45.0	22:20.0	27:55.0
34.0/68.0	1:42.0	2:16.0	2:50.0	4:15.0	5:40.0	8:30.0	11:20.0	14:10.0	17:00.0	22:40.0	28:20.0
34.5/69.0	1:43.5	2:18.0	2:52.5	4:18.8	5:45.0	8:37.5	11:30.0	14:22.5	17:15.0	23:00.0	28:45.0
35.0/70.0	1:45.0	2:20.0	2:55.0	4:22.5	5:50.0	8:45.0	11:40.0	14:35.0	17:30.0	23:20.0	29:10.0
35.5/71.0	1:46.5	2:22.0	2:57.5	4:26.3	5:55.0	8:52.5	11:50.0	14:47.5	17:45.0	23:40.0	29:35.0
36.0/72.0	1:48.0	2:24.0	3:00.0	4:30.0	6:00.0	9:00.0	12:00.0	15:00.0	18:00.0	24:00.0	30:00.0
36.5/73.0	1:49.5	2:26.0	3:02.5	4:33.8	6:05.0	9:07.5	12:10.0	15:12.5	18:15.0	24:20.0	30:25.0
37.0/74.0	1:51.0	2:28.0	3:05.0	4:37.5	6:10.0	9:15.0	12:20.0	15:25.0	18:30.0	24:40.0	30:50.0
37.5/75.0	1:52.5	2:30.0	3:07.5	4:41.3	6:15.0	9:22.5	12:30.0	15:37.5	18:45.0	25:00.0	31:15.0
38.0/76.0	1:54.0	2:32.0	3:10.0	4:45.0	6:20.0	9:30.0	12:40.0	15:50.0	19:00.0	25:20.0	31:40.0
38.5/77.0	1:55.5	2:34.0	3:12.5	4:48.8	6:25.0	9:37.5	12:50.0	16:02.5	19:15.0	25:40.0	32:05.0
39.0/78.0	1:57.0	2:36.0	3:15.0	4:52.5	6:30.0	9:45.0	13:00.0	16:15.0	19:30.0	26:00.0	32:30.0
39.5/79.0	1:58.5	2:38.0	3:17.5	4:56.3	6:35.0	9:52.5	13:10.0	16:27.5	19:45.0	26:20.0	32:55.0
40.0/80.0	2:00.0	2:40.0	3:20.0	5:00.0	6:40.0	10:00.0	13:20.0	16:40.0	20:00.0	26:40.0	33:20.0
40.5/81.0	2:01.5	2:42.0	3:22.5	5:03.8	6:45.0	10:07.5	13:30.0	16:52.5	20:15.0	27:00.0	33:45.0
41.0/82.0	2:03.0	2:44.0	3:25.0	5:07.5	6:50.0	10:15.0	13:40.0	17:05.0	20:30.0	27:20.0	34:10.0
41.5/83.0	2:04.5	2:46.0	3:27.5	5:11.3	6:55.0	10:22.5	13:50.0	17:17.5	20:45.0	27:40.0	34:35.0
42.0/84.0	2:06.0	2:48.0	3:30.0	5:15.0	7:00.0	10:30.0	14:00.0	17:30.0	21:00.0	28:00.0	35:00.0
42.5/85.0	2:07.5	2:50.0	3:32.5	5:18.8	7:05.0	10:37.5	14:10.0	17:42.5	21:15.0	28:20.0	35:25.0
43.0/86.0	2:09.0	2:52.0	3:35.0	5:22.5	7:10.0	10:45.0	14:20.0	17:55.0	21:30.0	28:40.0	35:50.0
43.5/87.0	2:10.5	2:54.0	3:37.5	5:26.3	7:15.0	10:52.5	14:30.0	18:07.5	21:45.0	29:00.0	36:15.0
44.0/88.0	2:12.0	2:56.0	3:40.0	5:30.0	7:20.0	11:00.0	14:40.0	18:20.0	22:00.0	29:20.0	36:40.0
44.5/89.0	2:13.5	2:58.0	3:42.5	5:33.8	7:25.0	11:07.5	14:50.0	18:32.5	22:15.0	29:40.0	37:05.0
45.0/90.0	2:15.0	3:00.0	3:45.0	5:37.5	7:30.0	11:15.0	15:00.0	18:45.0	22:30.0	30:00.0	37:30.0

Table 3: *Pace chart for track distances*

Examples (continued)

Day 3: 2 × 2000m @ 3000m pace.
Day 4: 4 × 600m @ 800m pace.

Another approach is to organise different paces during the same training session. This type of training session is particularly useful in developing the ability to cope with races in which the pace quickens as the race progresses.

Example:

2 × 600m +
3 × 400m +
4 × 200m

It is also possible to vary the speed within a repetition run to simulate changes of pace as they occur in a race. Repetition sessions to develop the ability to cope with variations in pace can be organised by inserting changes of pace into sessions.

1. *Simulating the second part of a race being run at a faster than race pace*
   Split each repetition into two halves, with the second half being run at a faster pace than the first. Examples:
   — 4 × 600m (2nd 300m 4-5 seconds faster than 1st 300m) with 4-5 mins recovery.
   — 4 × 1200m (2nd 600m faster than 1st 600m) with a 4-5 mins recovery.

2. *Simulating speed gradually increasing during the race*
   Split each repetition into three sections, each section run faster than the previous. Examples:
   — 3 × 600m (200m, 200m, 200m, each 1-2 secs faster than the previous) with a 10-15 mins recovery.
   — 2 × 3000m (1000m, 1000m, 1000m, each 4-5 secs faster than the previous) with a 15-20 mins recovery.

3. *Simulating a fast pace being injected in the middle of the race*
   Divide each repetition into three sections, with the first and third sections run at race pace and the middle section 2-3 seconds faster than race pace. Examples:
   — 2 × 1200m (400m, 400m, 400m, first and last 400m at race pace, middle 400m 2-3 secs faster).
   — 2 × 3000m (1000m, 1000m, 1000m, first and last 1000m at race pace, middle 1000m 4-5 secs faster).

4. *Sprint finish off a fast pace*
   Organise repetitions so that at some point in the last 100-200m of each run the runner lifts the pace and runs through the finishing line. Examples:
   — 4 × 800m at 1500m pace (accelerate at some point with 100m to 200m to go to finish line).
   — 3 × 1500m at 3000m pace (accelerate at some point with 200m to 600m to go to finish line).

The above are examples of how repetition sessions can be adjusted to help prepare for specific racing conditions. There are of course other racing scenarios which could equally be dealt with in this fashion.

Finishing speed

It is common for races to be won by a sprint finish. The sprint or run for the finishing line might be performed in the home straight or it may take the form of a long run for home, perhaps from as much as two laps out. The ability to sprint at full speed over a chosen distance despite the accompanying rapid build up of lactic acid needs to be developed. Runners need to practise sprinting over various distances with an accompanying build up of lactic acid to develop their ability to sprint at the end of a race.

At the end of a middle distance or steeplechase event, it is often the runner who can accelerate quickly and finish with a strong sprint finish who wins. The ability to sprint at the end of a race and tolerate high concentrations of lactic acid is called speed endurance. This ability is developed through fast runs over distances ranging from 150m up to 600m, allowing sufficient recovery to maintain quality throughout the session.

Speed Endurance
- Distances of 150m to 600m.
- Speeds corresponding to 85%-95% of best time for distance.
- Recoveries long enough to maintain quality of runs.

Specific Marathon Training

Specific training for the marathon differs from that of the other endurance running events as a result of the changes in energy source for this event. The main source of energy in all of the track events is carbohydrate. The marathon, however, requires in addition to carbohydrate, the utilisation of fat stores as a major fuel source. Most marathon runners are able to run at paces faster than their marathon pace for extended periods of time. Unfortunately these faster pace runs rely on carbohydrate as a fuel source and do not train the body to utilise fats. Specific training for the marathon involves extended runs at marathon pace or slower. This said, it is also important to include some training to develop aerobic power, maintain running speed and to develop a strong finish. Examples of specific marathon training are:

1. Long runs of 2-3 hours duration below race pace to encourage fat utilisation.
2. Long runs of up to 20 miles at race pace.
3. Interval runs such as 5 × 1 mile with a 2 min recovery.

Some coaches have replicated marathon conditions through combinations of training sessions similar to 2 and 3 above. An example would be undertaking a 20 mile run at marathon pace and then, after a rest period, running a faster 6 miles or even performing a session such as 6 × 1 mile with a short recovery. Such sessions are obviously demanding and should be used sparingly. Tables 4 and 5 offer a guide to the pace of marathon training sessions.

mile	2 miles	3 miles	4 miles	5 miles	6 miles
3:48					
3:52					
3:56					
4:00					
4:04					
4:08	8:16				
4:12	8:24				
4:16	8:32	12:48	17:04		
4:20	8:40	13:00	17:20		
4:24	8:48	13:12	17:36	22:00	26:24
4:28	8:56	13:24	17:52	22:20	26:48
4:32	9:04	13:36	18:08	22:40	27:12
4:36	9:12	13:48	18:24	23:00	27:36
4:40	9:20	14:00	18:40	23:20	28:00
4:44	9:28	14:12	18:56	23:40	28:24
4:48	9:36	14:24	19:12	24:00	28:48
4:52	9:44	14:36	19:28	24:20	29:12
4:56	9:52	14:48	19:44	24:40	29:36
5:00	10.00	15:00	20:00	25:00	30:00
5:04	10:08	15:12	20:16	25:20	30:24
5:08	10:16	15:24	20:32	25:40	30:48
5:12	10:24	15:36	20:48	26:00	31:12
5:16	10:32	15:48	21:04	26:20	31:36
5:20	10:40	16:00	21:20	26:40	32:00
5:24	10:48	16:12	21:36	27:00	32:24
5:28	10:56	16:24	21:52	27:20	32:48
5:32	11:04	16:36	22:08	27:40	33:12
5:36	11:12	16:48	22:24	28:00	33:36
5:40	11:20	17:00	22:40	28:20	34:00
5:44	11:28	17:24	22:56	28:40	34:24
5:48	11:36	17:36	23:12	29:00	34:48
5:52	11:44	17:48	23:28	29:20	35:12
5:56	11:52	17:48	23:44	29:40	35:36
6:00	12:00	18:00	24:00	30:00	36:00
6:04	12:08	18:12	24:16	30:20	36:24
6:08	12:16	18:24	24:32	30:40	36:48
6:12	12:24	18:36	24:48	31:00	37:12
6:16	12:32	18:48	25:04	31:20	37:36
6:20	12:40	19:00	25:20	31:40	38:00
6:24	12:48	19:12	25:36	32:00	38:24
6:28	12:56	19:36	25:52	32:20	38:48
6:32	13:04	19:36	26:08	32:40	39:12
6:36	13:12	19:48	26:24	33:00	39:36

Table 4: *Pace chart for 1-6 miles*

Mile pace	5 km (3.1mi)	5 miles	10 km (6.2mi)	15 km (9.3mi)	10 miles	20 km (12.4mi)	Half marathon	15 miles	25 km (15.5mi)	30 km (18.6mi)	20 miles	35 km (21.7mi)	40 km (24.8mi)	Marathon
4:40	14:30	23:20	29:00	43:30	46:40	58:00	1:01:11	1:10:00	1:12:30	1:27:00	1:33:20	1:41:30	1:56:00	2:02:22
4:45	14:46	23:45	29:31	44:17	47:30	59:02	1:02:17	1:11:15	1:13:48	1:28:33	1:35:00	1:43:19	1:58:04	2:04:33
4:50	15:01	24:10	30:02	45:03	48:20	1:00:04	1:03:22	1:12:30	1:15:05	1:30:06	1:36:40	1:45:07	2:00:08	2:06:44
4:55	15:17	24:35	30:33	45:50	49:10	1:01:06	1:04:28	1:13:45	1:16:23	1:31:39	1:38:20	1:46:56	2:02:12	2:08:55
5:00	15:32	25:00	31:04	46:36	50:00	1:02:08	1:05:33	1:15:00	1:17:40	1:33:12	1:40:00	1:48:44	2:04:16	2:11:06
5:05	15:48	25:25	31:35	47:23	50:50	1:03:10	1:06:39	1:16:15	1:18:58	1:34:45	1:41:40	1:50:33	2:06:20	2:13:17
5:10	16:03	25:50	32:06	48:09	51:40	1:04:12	1:07:44	1:17:30	1:20:15	1:36:18	1:43:20	1:52:21	2:08:24	2:15:28
5:15	16:19	26:15	32:37	48:56	52:30	1:05:14	1:08:50	1:18:45	1:21:33	1:37:51	1:45:00	1:54:10	2:10:28	2:17:39
5:20	16:34	26:40	33:08	49:42	53:20	1:06:16	1:09:55	1:20:00	1:22:50	1:39:24	1:46:40	1:55:58	2:12:32	2:19:50
5:25	16:50	27:05	33:39	50:29	54:10	1:07:18	1:11:01	1:21:15	1:24:08	1:40:57	1:48:20	1:57:47	2:14:36	2:22:01
5:30	17:05	27:30	34:10	51:15	55:00	1:08:20	1:12:06	1:22:30	1:25:25	1:42:30	1:50:00	1:59:35	2:16:40	2:24:12
5:35	17:21	27:55	34:41	52:02	55:50	1:09:22	1:13:12	1:23:45	1:26:43	1:44:03	1:51:40	2:01:24	2:18:44	2:26:23
5:40	17:36	28:20	35:12	52:48	56:40	1:10:24	1:14:17	1:25:00	1:28:00	1:45:36	1:53:20	2:03:12	2:20:48	2:28:34
5:45	17:52	28:45	35:43	53:35	57:30	1:11:26	1:15:23	1:26:15	1:29:18	1:47:09	1:55:00	2:05:01	2:22:52	2:30:45
5:50	18:07	29:10	36:14	54:21	58:20	1:12:28	1:16:28	1:27:30	1:30:35	1:48:42	1:56:40	2:06:49	2:24:56	2:32:56
5:55	18:23	29:35	36:45	55:08	59:10	1:13:30	1:17:34	1:28:45	1:31:53	1:50:15	1:58:20	2:08:38	2:27:00	2:35:07
6:00	18:38	30:00	37:16	55:54	1:00:00	1:14:32	1:18:39	1:30:00	1:33:10	1:51:48	2:00:00	2:10:26	2:29:04	2:37:18
6:05	18:54	30:25	37:47	56:41	1:00:50	1:15:34	1:19:45	1:31:15	1:34:28	1:53:21	2:01:40	2:12:15	2:31:08	2:39:29
6:10	19:09	30:50	38:18	57:27	1:01:40	1:16:36	1:20:50	1:32:30	1:35:45	1:54:54	2:03:20	2:14:03	2:33:12	2:41:40
6:15	19:25	31:15	38:49	58:14	1:02:30	1:17:38	1:21:56	1:33:45	1:37:03	1:56:27	2:05:00	2:15:52	2:35:16	2:43:51
6:20	19:40	31:40	39:20	59:00	1:03:20	1:18:40	1:23:01	1:35:00	1:38:20	1:58:00	2:06:40	2:17:40	2:37:20	2:46:02
6:25	19:56	32:05	39:51	59:47	1:04:10	1:19:42	1:24:07	1:36:15	1:39:38	1:59:33	2:08:20	2:19:29	2:39:24	2:48:13
6:30	20:11	32:30	40:22	1:00:33	1:05:00	1:20:44	1:25:12	1:37:30	1:40:55	2:01:06	2:10:00	2:21:17	2:41:28	2:50:24
6:35	20:27	32:55	40:53	1:01:20	1:05:50	1:21:46	1:26:18	1:38:45	1:42:13	2:02:39	2:11:40	2:23:06	2:43:32	2:52:35
6:40	20:42	33:20	41:24	1:02:06	1:06:40	1:22:48	1:27:23	1:40:00	1:43:30	2:04:12	2:13:20	2:24:54	2:45:36	2:54:46
6:45	20:58	33:45	41:55	1:02:53	1:07:30	1:23:50	1:28:29	1:41:15	1:44:48	2:05:45	2:15:00	2:26:43	2:47:40	2:56:57
6:50	21:13	34:10	42:26	1:03:39	1:08:20	1:24:52	1:29:34	1:42:30	1:46:05	2:07:18	2:16:40	2:28:31	2:49:44	2:59:08
6:55	21:29	34:35	42:57	1:04:26	1:09:10	1:25:54	1:30:40	1:43:45	1:47:23	2:08:51	2:18:20	2:30:20	2:51:48	3:01:19
7:00	21:44	35:00	43:28	1:05:12	1:10:00	1:26:56	1:31:45	1:45:00	1:48:40	2:10:24	2:20:00	2:32:08	2:53:52	3:03:30
7:05	22:00	35:25	43:59	1:05:59	1:10:50	1:27:58	1:32:51	1:46:15	1:49:58	2:11:57	2:21:40	2:33:57	2:55:56	3:05:41
7:10	22:15	35:50	44:30	1:06:45	1:11:40	1:29:00	1:33:56	1:47:30	1:51:15	2:13:30	2:23:20	2:35:45	2:58:00	3:07:52
7:15	22:31	36:15	45:01	1:07:32	1:12:30	1:30:02	1:35:02	1:48:45	1:52:33	2:15:03	2:25:00	2:37:34	3:00:04	3:10:03
7:20	22:46	36:40	45:32	1:08:18	1:13:20	1:31:04	1:36:07	1:50:00	1:53:50	2:16:36	2:26:40	2:39:22	3:02:08	3:12:14
7:25	23:02	37:05	46:03	1:09:05	1:14:10	1:32:06	1:37:13	1:51:15	1:55:08	2:18:09	2:28:20	2:41:11	3:04:12	3:14:25
7:30	23:17	37:30	46:34	1:09:51	1:15:00	1:33:08	1:38:18	1:52:30	1:56:25	2:19:42	2:30:00	2:42:59	3:06:16	3:16:36
7:35	23:33	37:55	47:05	1:10:38	1:15:50	1:34:10	1:39:24	1:53:45	1:57:43	2:21:15	2:31:40	2:44:48	3:08:20	3:18:47
7:40	23:48	38:20	47:36	1:11:24	1:16:40	1:35:12	1:40:29	1:55:00	1:59:00	2:22:48	2:33:20	2:46:36	3:10:24	3:20:58
7:45	24:04	38:45	48:07	1:12:11	1:17:30	1:36:14	1:41:35	1:56:15	2:00:18	2:24:21	2:35:00	2:48:25	3:12:28	3:23:09
7:50	24:19	39:10	48:38	1:12:57	1:18:20	1:37:16	1:42:40	1:57:30	2:01:35	2:25:54	2:36:40	2:50:13	3:14:32	3:25:20
7:55	24:35	39:35	49:09	1:13:44	1:19:10	1:38:18	1:43:46	1:58:45	2:02:53	2:27:27	2:38:20	2:52:02	3:16:36	3:27:31

Table 5: *Pace chart for the marathon*

23

CHAPTER 3

DEVELOPING MOBILITY AND STRENGTH

Training which improves the middle and long distance runner's endurance is given the highest priority in the athlete's training plan. Other forms of training, although contributing less to the competitive performance, also have an important place in an athlete's programme. Mobility and strength training do not improve that runner's endurance capacities, but do play a key role in protecting against injury and in contributing to speed development.

Mobility and strength training in the endurance runner's programme therefore have two major objectives:

1. To increase the range of movement and general strength of areas of the body which are prone to injury in order to protect them.

2. To improve factors such as range of movement, strength, strength endurance and elastic strength which contribute to the runner's competitive performance.

MOBILITY

Mobility training involves exercises which aim to stretch selected muscles and their connective tissues. It is muscle and the tissues which surround and attach muscle to bone that limit the range of movement of the various joint actions which facilitate the running and hurdling actions. The activities which stretch these muscles are often referred to as stretching, flexibility or suppleness exercises, the aim of each exercise being to stretch to the limit of the range of movement, often referred to as the end position, and to seek to improve the range by stretching at and beyond this point.

Increasing the length of muscles and their connective tissues plays an important role in assisting endurance athletes to avoid injury successfully.

The term mobility refers to the capacity to perform joint actions through a wide range of movement. A runner with good mobility will possess an adequate range of movement in the shoulder, hip and ankle joints allowing a full running stride to be achieved. This in turn will improve speed by allowing an optimal stride length when sprinting at full speed, and at sub maximal speeds will allow an economical running action. Efficiency in clearing the barriers will be enhanced where steeplechasers possess good hip mobility.

Mobility Training

There are a number of techniques used in performing mobility exercises to increase your range of movement. The simplest and safest is the active or slow stretch method. A number of mobility exercises are illustrated, all of which can be performed using the active method.

In the active method, exercises are performed by slowly stretching as shown in the illustration to the end of the range of movement (until a slight stiffness or pain is felt). This position should then be held for about 10-15 seconds. The stretch is then released; you relax and then repeat the exercise a number of times. When holding the stretched position other parts of the body should be as relaxed as possible. It also helps to concentrate on relaxing the muscles which are being stretched.

Greater mobility can be achieved in warm rather than cold conditions. It is therefore important that the runner increases the heat in his muscles through light running or jogging before stretching. In cold conditions it will be necessary to wear warm clothing whilst stretching, but care must be taken to ensure that tight clothing does not restrict movement. Mobility training is best undertaken in a warm environment which usually means indoors in our climate.

Most runners undertake mobility exercises as part of their warm-up activities, but even when a specific unit of mobility training is to be included in a training session it should precede other forms of training. This applies especially to high quality aerobic and anaerobic endurance training as there is a strong body of opinion that mobility work should never follow exercise which causes local muscular fatigue.

Some coaches do however advocate stretching activity as part of the warm down at the end of a training session. If mobility work is to form part of the warm down, exercises should be performed with care as there is a danger in stretching fatigued muscles. Only careful slow stretching exercises should be used.

Mobility Exercises

The following exercises have been broken into three groups. The first are a series of all round mobility exercises which can form the basis of a warm-up session. The second group are a series of specific exercises designed to stretch muscle groups which play an important role in running and may need special attention. The third and final group is a set of exercises for hurdlers aimed at those runners participating in the steeplechase.

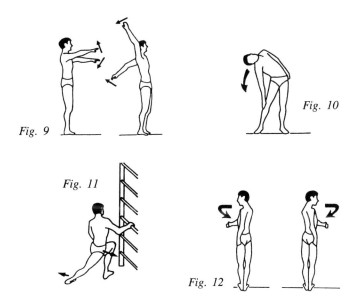

Fig. 9

Fig. 10

Fig. 11

Fig. 12

Figs. 9-12 General mobility exercises.

Fig. 13

Fig. 14

Fig. 15

Fig. 16

Fig. 17

Fig. 18

Fig. 19

Fig. 20(a)

Fig. 20(b)

Figs. 13-20 General mobility exercises.

Fig. 21

Fig. 22

Fig. 23

Fig. 24

Fig. 25

Fig. 26

Fig. 27

Figs. 21-30 Specific mobility exercises.

Fig. 29

Fig. 28

Fig. 30

Fig. 31

Fig. 32

Fig. 33

Fig. 34

Fig. 35

Fig. 36

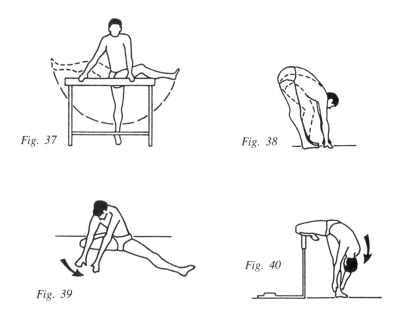

Fig. 37

Fig. 38

Fig. 39

Fig. 40

Figs. 31-40 Mobility exercises for steeplechase.

STRENGTH

Not all runners include strength exercises in their training, arguing that time is better spent developing endurance. Whilst one could not argue that endurance is the key training factor in the runner's programme, time invested in strength training may save time lost through injury and in certain cases may contribute to performance in a positive manner.

Strength training makes its most significant contribution to speed development, a quality required by all runners. The shorter the competitive distance the greater the importance of speed and therefore strength development. Strength is therefore arguably more important in 800m/1500m running than 5K/10K running, and more important in 5K/10K running than marathon. Strength may be more important in the 3000m steeplechase than in the 3000m flat. The steeplechase demands a fair degree of strength and strength endurance in order that runners can cope with the clearance of barriers and water jumps.

Some male distance runners possess good levels of natural strength, whilst others are not as strong and need to develop this aspect of conditioning. Female runners have lower levels of strength than men and they do need to include strength work in their programmes.

A number of common injuries associated with running can be prevented by the use of strength exercises. Running tends to develop strength in the major muscle groups of the legs such as the hip, knee and ankle extensors. Other muscle groups providing a supporting role are neglected and their weakness is often the cause of injury. Preventative strength work will improve the strength and the local endurance of selected muscles.

Preventative Strength

The following exercises strengthen supporting muscle groups and have an important role to play in the runner's programme, protecting him/her against potential injury.

Straight Leg Raise

Fig. 41

Purpose: Strengthens the internal vast thigh muscle which is important for knee stability. Protects against "runner's knee" or chondromalacia patella.

◄ *Description:* Sit on a box or chair. Lift and straighten one leg as shown. From this starting position raise the straight leg. Repeat exercise on other leg. Once strength is developed, increase load by adding an ankle weight.

Heel Lower and Raise

Purpose: Strengthens and stretches the achilles tendon.

Description: Stand on block or step as shown. Gently lower heel, then raise. Once strength has developed, use weights machine or free weight to increase resistance.

Fig. 42(a)   *Fig. 42(b)*

Shin Strengthener

Purpose: Strengthens small muscle groups down front of shin and protects against "shin splints".

◄ *Description:* Sit on a box or high stool as shown. Pull toes up towards shin (dorsi-flexion) and hold. Repeat with other leg.

Fig. 43

Abdominal Crunch

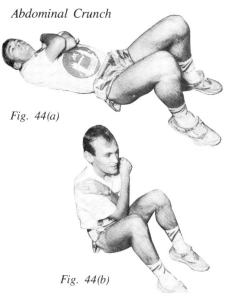

Fig. 44(a)

Fig. 44(b)

Purpose: To strengthen the abdominal muscles. Takes pressure off lower back.

Description: Lying on back. Bend knees, feet flat on ground. Arms across chest. Gently curl chest up towards thighs. When exercise becomes easier towards end of roll-up, slowly roll back down. Make sure that feet are not anchored and that legs remain bent. Make easier by reaching forward with hands. Make harder and recruit oblique muscles by including a twisting action to each side. Can also be made harder by asking athlete to hold a weights disk.

Back Raise

Fig. 45(a)

Fig. 45(b)

Purpose: To strengthen the extensor and rotational muscles of the back.

Description: Legs and hips supported on box or similar. Trunk leaning over the box. Raise trunk until just beyond parallel to the ground. Ensure that head is kept in natural alignment by continuing to look at the ground. Cross arms over chest and, if additional loading is required, hold weights disk in arms.

Hamstring Curl

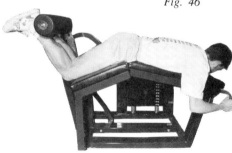

Fig. 46

Purpose: To strengthen the hamstring muscles.

Description: Using a hamstring curl machine, flex knee to bring heels up towards buttocks and then lower. Keep weight light and perform reasonably quickly. Possible to exercise one leg at a time. Ensure an angled bench and avoid hips being raised off bench during exercise.

Leg Side Raise

Purpose: To strengthen the small and medium buttock muscles (Abductor Muscles).

Description: Lying on side raise leg. Use ankle weights to increase work load.

Fig. 47

Adductor Strengthener

Purpose: To strengthen the adductor muscles of the leg.

Description: Standing with knees bent, squeeze ball between knees.

Fig. 48

GENERAL STRENGTH TRAINING
Circuit & Stage Training

Circuit training and stage training are useful methods of structuring general all-round strength training programmes. With both systems general strength and local muscular endurance can be developed. This is especially relevant to the muscles of the trunk and arms in which a lack of local muscular endurance can limit performance through problems such as stitches.

Circuit training involves about six to eight exercises set out in a circuit. The runner performs one set of one exercise and then moves on to the next and so on until all exercises have been completed. Having completed one circuit, the athlete sets out on a second circuit. Normally three to six circuits would be included in one training session.

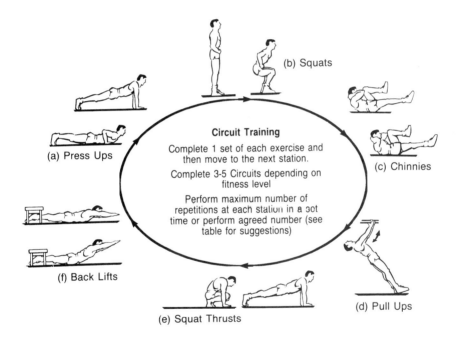

Circuit Training

Complete 1 set of each exercise and then move to the next station.

Complete 3-5 Circuits depending on fitness level

Perform maximum number of repetitions at each station in a set time or perform agreed number (see table for suggestions)

(a) Press Ups
(b) Squats
(c) Chinnies
(d) Pull Ups
(e) Squat Thrusts
(f) Back Lifts

Press Ups	Squats	Chinnies	Pull Ups	Squat Thrusts	Back Lifts
12 Reps	20 Reps	30 Reps	6 Reps	15 Reps	10 Reps

Fig. 49 Circuit training.

The period of recovery between exercises in circuit training is the time it takes to complete a circuit. To make training more demanding a shorter recovery is necessary. The exercises can therefore be conducted in the form of stage training where all sets of an exercise are completed with a short recovery interval before moving on to the next exercise.

A good way of organising sessions is to combine exercises using one exercise as the recovery period for the other. In this way all the sets of two exercises are completed before moving on to the next two exercises. This system has the effect of halving the time required for stage training.

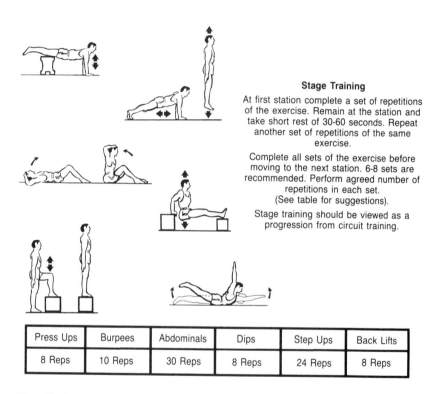

Stage Training

At first station complete a set of repetitions of the exercise. Remain at the station and take short rest of 30-60 seconds. Repeat another set of repetitions of the same exercise.

Complete all sets of the exercise before moving to the next station. 6-8 sets are recommended. Perform agreed number of repetitions in each set.
(See table for suggestions).

Stage training should be viewed as a progression from circuit training.

Press Ups	Burpees	Abdominals	Dips	Step Ups	Back Lifts
8 Reps	10 Reps	30 Reps	8 Reps	24 Reps	8 Reps

Fig. 50 Stage training.

Weight Training

Weight Training can be used to develop maximal strength, elastic strength or strength endurance depending on the chosen number of sets and repetitions. Training can make use of free weights such as Olympic bars, barbells and dumbells or fixed weights such as multi-gym machines. Repetitions of between 1 and 5 will develop maximal strength, repetitions of about 5 or 6 performed at speed will develop elastic strength and repetitions of 10-20 will develop strength endurance.

The exercises shown here would form the basis of a middle distance runner's weight training programme. There are three main exercises which make up the core of a weight training programme:

1. Back Squat

Fig. 51(a)

Fig. 51(b)

2. Power Clean

Fig. 52(a)

Fig. 52(b)

3. Bench Press

Fig. 53(a)

Fig. 53(b)

These can be added to by other exercises such as heel raises, hamstring curls, abdominal raises, back extensions, arm curls, tricep curls, etc. Normally, an athlete would perform 4-5 sets of these different exercises using about six exercises in one session, the three main lifts plus three others.

Bicep Curl

Fig. 54(a)

Fig. 54(b)

Press Behind Neck

Arm Extension

Fig. 55(a)

Fig. 55(b)

Fig. 56

Resistance Runs

Various forms of resistance running exist which require the runner to exert force through the running action against an increased load. These methods can be used to develop both strength endurance and elastic strength. Common methods include sprinting up hills or sand dunes, running with additional weight using weighted jackets, ankle weights or weights carried in the hands and running whilst pulling a resistance. These activities are discussed in the previous chapter under strength endurance training.

(a)

(b)

(c)

Fig. 57 Resistance running (a: hill running; b: towing; c: weighted jacket).

Elastic Strength Exercises

When running, the foot is only in contact with the ground for a fraction of a second. During this short period of time, the runner has to apply force to the ground to propel himself forwards. The ability to apply force over a short period of time is called power or elastic strength. Exercises to develop this aspect of strength include a range of hopping, jumping and bounding activities. Used over extended distances, these activities may also develop strength endurance.

Fig. 58 Bounding.

Fig. 59 Touch-off skipping.

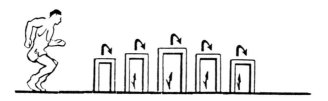

Fig. 60 Hurdle jumps.

CHAPTER 4

DEVELOPING SKILL AND SPEED

The Running Action

The running action can be considered under three headings:

— Movement of Legs
— Posture of Torso
— Movement of Arms

Movement of Legs

The running action of the legs consists of the *driving phase* and the *recovery phase*. The driving phase commences when the foot first contacts the ground during the running stride. The runner's bodyweight is supported by the foot whilst his hips pass over the foot, after which the hip, knee and ankle extend to push the runner forwards.

The recovery phase commences as the runner's foot leaves the ground. The heel is pulled upwards towards the buttocks, folding the leg into a short and fast moving lever. At the same time, the thigh is swung through bringing the thigh parallel to the ground. The lower leg then reaches forwards with the foot cocked as the thigh starts to move downwards. The foot, lower leg and thigh are then swept backwards and downwards creating an active striking action. The foot meets the ground lightly, striking it with the outside edge of the ball of the foot. The foot then rolls towards the inside, bringing the whole of the ball of the foot into contact with the ground.

Posture of Torso

The trunk remains almost erect with only a slight lean forwards. There should be no twisting or rotating of the torso during running. It should remain square to the direction of running, providing a strong structure to link together the coordinated actions of the arms and legs. The neck should be relaxed, with the head held in natural alignment and with the eyes looking straight ahead.

Movement of Arms

The arms coordinate with the action of the legs. As a leg drives against the ground it is matched by the opposite driving arm. Each arm is coordinated with the opposite leg in order to balance the athlete as he runs.

The angle of the elbow changes as the arms swing backwards and forwards. They should, in full flight running, be at right angles at the rear and front of the swinging action. The hands should be kept relaxed and lightly cupped, with the thumbs resting on the fingers. The elbows brush the sides as the arms swing backwards and forwards. The shoulders are held low and relaxed. Swinging movements should be in line with the direction of running, although most women's cross slightly towards the centre line of the body.

See Fig. 61: overleaf

Fig. 61 Running action — Steve Cram, G.B.

Economical Running

Endurance runners need to run economically for parts of their competitive events in order to conserve energy. They can also be required to accelerate quickly to full flight running at top speed as they sprint for the finishing line or in making a tactical break. When running economically the runner's stride length decreases; his driving action will not be as vigorous and the thigh may not be picked up as much as in full flight running. The range of movement of the arms, which is linked to the stride length, also shortens.

The slower the running speed, the flatter the foot as it contacts the ground. In some cases, for example when out on a long training run, the foot may even strike the ground heel first.

Key Technical Points

Running technique can be developed whilst athletes are running at a speed which is fast enough to require a full running action but is not top speed. This type of running occurs in the warm-up strides and whilst performing interval or repetition work on the track. During such training, technique can also be developed by asking the runner to concentrate on a particular aspect whilst running. Seven key points to focus on have been identified and these are detailed below together with *trigger phrases* intended to relay the feel of the aspect of technique to the athlete.

1. *Running Tall* (Figure 62)

   Head in clouds. Hips high. Grow two inches. Upright. Running proud. Up on balls of feet.

2. *High Thighs* (Figure 63)

   Lift knees. Lift thighs. Squeeze thigh higher. Thigh high. High front arm. Lift.

3. *Rear Leg Extension* (Figure 64)

   Leave foot on track. Push track away. Push off toe.

4. *Relaxation* (Figure 65)

   Low shoulders. Push shoulders low. Smile. Hands curled. Hands loose. Light grip. Run loose. Head on shoulders. Look straight ahead.

5. *Run in a Straight Line* (Figure 66)

   Elbows in. Feet straight. Arms swing from shoulders.

6. *Rear Elbow Drive* (Figure 67)

   Drive elbow back. Pull/squeeze elbow back. Shoulders low and square.

7. *Active Strike* (Figure 68)

   Clawing action. Pawing action. Reach and pull foot back to strike ground and push away.

Running Drills

In addition to developing technique whilst the athlete runs, there are a number of drills which develop aspects of the running action. These involve walking, jogging and skipping activities.

Fig. 62 Running tall.

Fig. 63 High thighs.

Fig. 64 Rear leg extension.

Fig. 65 Relaxed running.

Fig. 66 Straight line running.

Fig. 67 Rear elbow drive.

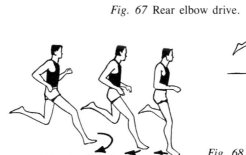

Fig. 68 Active strike.

1. *High Knee Drill* (Figure 69)

   Thigh is picked up to a position parallel to ground with ankle and knee flexed. Emphasise tall body position, up on toes, active landing of foot and use of arms. Exercise can be performed as a walking drill, skipping drill or a jogging drill.

2. *Recovery Leg Action* (Figure 70)

   Foot is picked up towards buttock and thigh is pulled through. The feeling is of the leg folding up. Emphasise tall body position, up on toes and use of arms. Exercise can be used as a walking or running drill.

3. *Bounding* (Figure 71)

   The action of bounding is similar to that of running, but it involves leaping from one foot to the other which delays the action, allowing aspects of technique to be emphasised. Focus on good rear leg extension and a high thigh pick up at the front. Also encourage an active foot strike and good use of the arms. Bounding can also be used as a good strengthening exercise.

Fig. 69 High knee drill.

Fig. 70 Recovery leg action.

Fig. 71 Bounding.

The Hurdling Action

The object of the technique used to clear the hurdle is to allow the runner to clear the barrier in one stride with the minimum interruption to his running speed or rhythm. As with the normal running action, the technique of clearing the hurdle can be described under the following three headings:

— Movement of Legs
— Posture of Torso
— Movement of Arms

Movement of Legs

As the runner approaches the hurdle he will pick out the barrier and make small adjustments to his running stride in order that he takes off a suitable distance from the hurdle. This ability, which is called spatial judgement, develops with practice but can diminish as the steeplechaser fatigues. In taking off the correct distance from the hurdle, the athlete picks up his lead leg bent and high. The result of this movement is that his hip is pulled in towards the hurdle, allowing good drive from the pushing action of the driving leg. The lead leg then opens up as the heel is driven across the top of the hurdle. As the steeplechaser passes over the barrier, the whole leading leg is quickly pulled back down in order that the foot can contact the ground as soon and as actively as possible. If observed from the front, the lead leg would be seen to be picked up and placed back down on the track in a straight line.

The object of pulling the foot back down quickly is so that, as the steeplechaser passes over the foot, he can drive away from the barrier without loss of speed. The drive over the hurdle is created by the rear leg, which then has to be brought across the hurdle and round to the front in order to take the first running stride away from the barrier. This is done by pulling the heel of the trail leg to the buttock at the same time as pulling the knee up towards the arm-pit. As the trail leg rises, it is then pulled across the top of the barrier and round the front of the body into a sprinting position.

Posture of the Torso

Maintenance of speed across the hurdle is assisted if the steeplechaser leans slightly in towards the barrier prior to running over it. This encourages forward motion, allows the trail leg to be brought across the hurdle and assists the steeplechaser in running off the barrier.

Movement of Arms

The arms are coordinated with the actions of the legs. As the steeplechaser picks up his lead knee and leans slightly into the hurdle, the opposite arm acts as a balance by reaching across the hurdle. The other arm is held by the side. As the steeplechaser passes over the barrier, the lead arm is brought down and back into the sprinting action. The other arm is held by the side until the trail leg starts to come round to the front, when it is brought up into the sprinting action to balance the trail leg action.

Technical Training

Hurdling is best learned using normal hurdles as opposed to steeplechase barriers. Hurdles can be lowered, allowing the runner to learn the technique gradually. The runner should be asked to run over four or five hurdles placed so that he can take 3, 5 or 7 strides between, allowing each hurdle to be taken with the same lead leg. To develop the use of an alternate lead leg, distances which correspond with 4, 6 and 8 strides can be used. He should be encouraged to run over the hurdles and not to jump them. The height of the barriers is

Fig. 72 Steeplechase barrier technique — Ivan Konovalov, USSR

46

gradually raised to the regulation 3 feet, stopping at intermediate heights if the runner starts to jump the barrier. At the first height where the runner finds clearing the barrier difficult, the coach will instruct on barrier clearance emphasising the key points of technique.

Key Points of Hurdling Technique

1. Pick up and place lead leg back down in a straight line.
2. Lead leg knee picked up bent, heel drives across hurdle, leg brought back down to ground quickly.
3. Trail leg is brought round the side, pulled across the hurdle as a short lever with knee flexed and heel tucked in.
4. The knee of the trail leg is pulled across the body high into the sprint position with the heel held in tight.
5. The runner leans into the barrier.
6. The arm opposite the lead leg reaches across the hurdle and is then brought down and back.
7. The arm opposite the trail leg is held by the side, and then moves forward into a sprinting action to balance the pull through of the trail leg.
8. The runner must pick out each barrier and run over it.

Hurdle Drills

The lead leg and trail leg action can be developed using a variety of static, walking, jogging and running drills. The drills below are a sample of such drills. Further training practices can be found in the BAAB booklet on hurdling.

1. *Walk Over Drill* (Figure 73)
   Place several hurdles 1-1.5 metres apart and ask runner to walk over them. Emphasise walking with high hips, on toes, pick up lead leg knee high and bent, place straight back down, use arms in hurdling action, trail leg is picked up high and brought round to front before being lowered.

2. *Lead Leg Drill* (Figure 74)
   Runner walks down side of hurdles performing lead leg action over each barrier. This can then be developed into a jog down the side or a run. Hurdles can be spaced to allow three or five strides.

Fig. 73 Hurdle walk over drill.   *Fig. 74* Lead leg drill.

3. *Trail Leg Drill* (Figure 75)
   Same as for lead leg but isolating trail leg.

Water Jump Technique

In the water jump technique, the runner places his foot on top of the barrier and drives across the water. The technique involves picking out the barrier

Fig. 76 Water jump technique — Colin Reitz, G.B.

and adjusting strides so that the steeplechaser can get close enough to allow a good drive onto the hurdle. In a similar manner to hurdling, he leans in, drives up and forwards with a bent knee. The lead foot is firmly placed on the top of the barrier and the steeplechaser keeps his centre of gravity low as he passes over the top. This allows him to maintain horizontal speed and prepares for a good drive over the water. A good drive is achieved by the foot pushing vigorously off the edge of the barrier ensuring full leg extension. The free knee is picked up high to limit forward rotation and the steeplechaser clears most of the water with a good split position. The foot of the leg now leading lands towards the top of the slope of the water jump. As a consequence this foot lands in the water. The foot of the driving leg is then brought through to strike the track outside the water. The steeplechaser can then step out of the water and continue running without breaking his running rhythm. A key factor in a successful clearance of the water jump is keeping the centre of gravity low as he passes over the barrier.

Technical Training

This technique is best taught initially using a steeplechase barrier and the long jump pit. A barrier can be placed across the long jump runway in front of the pit. The runner can then run down the runway and practise the technique, landing in the sand. This saves having to fill the water jump with water.

Key Points of Technique

1. Get close enough to barrier to allow good drive. Lean into the barrier, drive up and forwards with a bent knee.
2. Place foot firmly on top of hurdle.
3. Keep centre of gravity low over the barrier.
4. Achieve a good split by keeping foot in contact with top of barrier and driving out across water.
5. Pick up knee to achieve good split and to counter rotation.
6. Land with first foot in water, and second taking first stride away from water.

Speed

Running speed is the product of stride length and stride rate. An improvement in either factor will lead to improved speed. The technique work outlined earlier in this section, together with improved mobility and strength, will develop stride length. Stride rate can be developed through a number of activities including some of the speed drills outlined below:

Speed Drills

1. *"Pitter Patter" Drill* (Figure 77)

   Jogging drill performed with quick leg movements. Emphasise ankle extension and flexion. Runner slowly moves along ground for about 30 metres, but moves legs quickly trying to achieve as many movements of the legs as possible in the time he takes to complete the 30m. Runner "pitter patters" along the ground.

2. *Prancing Drill* (Figure 78)

   Jogging drill also performed with quick leg movements. Knees picked up to half height and then foot returns to ground quickly. Runner moves slowly over 30m achieving as many leg movements as possible.

Fig. 77 Pitter-patter drill.

Fig. 78 Prancing drill.

3. *Touch-Off Skipping Drill* (Figure 79)

Skipping drill for about 30 metres. Fast touch-off skipping action used. As soon as foot contacts ground it is lifted off again. Use arms and legs in action similar to high knee lift technique drill, but emphasise speed of foot movement off the ground as opposed to range of movement emphasised in technique drills.

Fig. 79 Touch-off skipping drill.

Sprinting

Speed can be developed by encouraging both stride rate and stride length through sprint work on the track. This training will involve sprinting over a variety of distances at or close to full sprinting speed. Such training usually takes place at the beginning of a training session in order that the runners are fresh and good recoveries are taken to avoid fatigue.

Some example sessions are:

1. Sprinting from a rolling or standing start over distances of 40m to 80m with a walk back recovery. 8-12 repetitions organised in sets, e.g. 2 × 4 × 60m with a walk back recovery and 10 minutes between sets.

2. Acceleration runs over distances of 60m-120m. Runner gradually builds up speed until running last 20m or so at full speed, e.g. 6 × 120m acceleration runs with a jog back recovery.

3. Split pace runs where the runner covers part distance at steady speed and then, on reaching a point, accelerates to top speed. Distances of 120m to 150m used, e.g. 6 × 150m with 75m at steady speed and 75m accelerating to top speed.

Specific Speed

Speed sessions which incorporate a gradual build-up of speed, such as the acceleration runs or split pace runs, can be used at the end of training sessions. Although their contribution at this point of the session will not develop speed as well as it would if the athlete were fresh, it does educate the athlete to produce and maintain full flight running even when tired. Simple sprint sessions such as those outlined in 1 above are not suited to this type of work.

CHAPTER 5

PLANNING TRAINING

Success in endurance running events results from consistent training over a period of time, sometimes several years. It is also the product of careful short and long term planning. This chapter outlines the process of planning training and presents examples of training programmes.

The Planning Process

The planning of training is an on-going process which involves the assessment, planning and implementation of training programmes. Before training programmes can be planned, an assessment of the current status of the runner needs to be made along with an evaluation of the demands of the runner's event and competition programme. With this information decisions can be made regarding the structure and content of the runner's training programme. The programme can then be written, implemented and of course continually re-evaluated, for planning is an on-going process.

The first step in the planning of training programmes is to assess the runner's current status in terms of performance level, conditioning and skills, as well as assessing the availability of facilities and support. The pre-training checklist (see Table 6) is a useful means of collecting key information. The coach meets with his athlete prior to planning an annual training plan and uses the checklist as a method of ensuring that all important information has been assembled before commencing the writing of schedules.

1.00 **PERSONAL DETAILS**
1.01 Name
1.02 Date of birth
1.03 Address(es)
1.04 Telephone number(s)
1.05 Height

2.00 **ANNUAL GOALS**
2.01 Competitive goals (expected results in competition)
2.02 Performance goals (times)
2.03 Technical goals (technique/tactics improvement)
2.04 Conditioning goals (conditioning improvement)

3.00 **PREVIOUS EXPERIENCE**
3.01 Personal bests
3.02 Club
3.03 Former coaching
3.04 Current training

4.00 **COMMITMENTS AND TIME AVAILABLE FOR TRAINING**
4.01 Academic/work background
4.02 Family background
4.03 Hobbies/other sports
4.04 Time available for training

5.00 **MEDICAL BACKGROUND**
5.01 Previous injuries
5.02 Previous illness
5.03 Current problems (allergies/epilepsy/diabetes)
5.04 Access to medical support

6.00 **AVAILABILITY OF TRAINING FACILITIES**
6.01 Tracks
6.02 Other running facilities
6.03 Gymnasia
6.04 Weight training
6.05 Active recovery (saunas, swimming pools, massage, etc.)

7.00 **DIET**
7.01 General eating habits
7.02 Supplements
7.03 Drinking habits

8.00 **TWO KEY QUESTIONS**
8.01 How serious are you about your athletics?
8.02 What do you expect from me as a coach?

Table 6: *The Pre-training checklist.*

The next step is to set annual goals with the runner. These can include:

1. *Competition Goals* — The main competitions of the year and what the runner hopes to achieve in them.
2. *Performance Goals* — The times the runner hopes to achieve during the year.
3. *Conditioning Goals* — Those aspects of conditioning the runner hopes to develop and to what level.
4. *Skill Goals* — Those aspects of technique or tactics that the runner hopes to develop.

Like all other goals these should be challenging, realistic, achievable and easily measurable.

Having set goals with the runner and prior to mapping out the annual plan, thought should be given to the demands of the runner's event and the demands of the envisaged competition programme. There are differences in approach to preparing an athlete to compete for each of the endurance events. The demands of running an 800m differ greatly from running a 5000m, which in turn differs greatly from running the marathon. Thought also needs to be given to the nature of the runner's major competitions. Are they one-off races such as a marathon, or are they a series of races held over a short period of time such as in track events at a major games.

Annual Training Plans
Using an annual year planner such as the one shown in Figure 83, the runner's major and minor competitions are then located. Once this is done, it is then possible to divide the year up into periods of preparation and recovery.

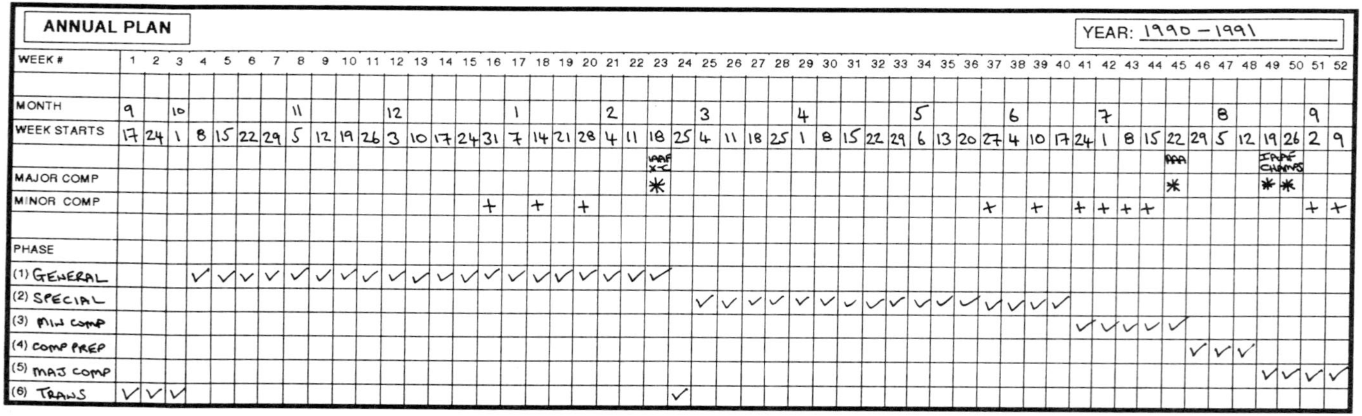

Fig. 80 Annual training plan — cross-country/outdoor track.

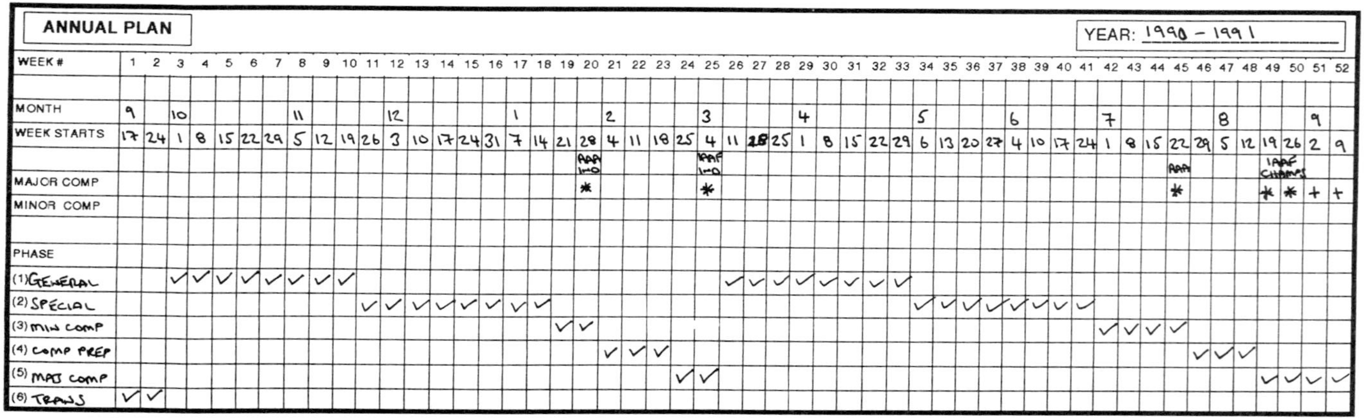

ANNUAL PLAN																																																			YEAR: 1990 – 1991
WEEK #	1	2	3	4	5	6	7	8	9	10	11	12	13	14	15	16	17	18	19	20	21	22	23	24	25	26	27	28	29	30	31	32	33	34	35	36	37	38	39	40	41	42	43	44	45	46	47	48	49	50	51	52
MONTH	9		10				11					12					1				2				3				4				5				6				7				8				9			
WEEK STARTS	17	24	1	8	15	22	29	5	12	19	26	3	10	17	24	31	7	14	21	28	4	11	18	25	1	8	15	22	29	6	13	20	27	6	13	20	27	10	17	24	1	8	15	22	29	5	12	19	26	2	9	
MAJOR COMP																							✻																					✻			✻					
MINOR COMP			+											+		+	+			+									+				✶			+		+			+		+	+			+			+	+

Fig. 81 Annual training plan — indoor track/outdoor track.

ANNUAL PLAN																																																			YEAR: 1990 – 1991
WEEK #	1	2	3	4	5	6	7	8	9	10	11	12	13	14	15	16	17	18	19	20	21	22	23	24	25	26	27	28	29	30	31	32	33	34	35	36	37	38	39	40	41	42	43	44	45	46	47	48	49	50	51	52
MONTH	9		10				11					12					1				2				3				4				5				6				7				8				9			
WEEK STARTS	17	24	1	8	15	22	29	5	12	19	26	3	10	17	24	31	7	14	21	28	4	11	18	25	1	8	15	22	25	1	8	15	22	6	13	20	27	4	10	17	24	1	8	15	22	29	5	12	19	26	2	9
MAJOR COMP																				✻				✶																				✻			✶		✶			
MINOR COMP																																																			+	+

ANNUAL PLAN   YEAR: 1990 – 1991

WEEK #	1	2	3	4	5	6	7	8	9	10	11	12	13	14	15	16	17	18	19	20	21	22	23	24	25	26	27	28	29	30	31	32	33	34	35	36	37	38	39	40	41	42	43	44	45	46	47	48	49	50	51	52
MONTH	11				12				1				2				3				4					5				6			7			8					9				10							
WEEK STARTS	5	12	19	26	3	10	17	24	31	7	14	21	28	4	11	18	25	1	8	15	22	29	8	15	22	29	6	13	20	27	4	10	17	24	1	8	15	22	29	5	12	19	26	2	9	16	23	30	7	14	21	28
MAJOR COMP																								*																												*
MINOR COMP																							3½/																													
PHASE																																																				
(1) GENERAL	✓	✓	✓	✓	✓	✓	✓	✓	✓	✓	✓	✓	✓																																							
(2) SPECIFIC														✓	✓	✓	✓	✓	✓	✓	✓	✓					✓	✓	✓	✓	✓	✓	✓	✓	✓	✓	✓	✓	✓	✓	✓	✓	✓								
(3) COMP																																																			✓	✓
(4) TRANS																							✓	✓		✓	✓																										
(5)																																																					
(6)																																																					

Fig. 82 Annual training plan — marathon.

ANNUAL PLAN   YEAR: _____

WEEK #	1	2	3	4	5	6	7	8	9	10	11	12	13	14	15	16	17	18	19	20	21	22	23	24	25	26	27	28	29	30	31	32	33	34	35	36	37	38	39	40	41	42	43	44	45	46	47	48	49	50	51	52
MONTH																																																					
WEEK STARTS																																																					
MAJOR COMP																																																					
MINOR COMP																																																					
PHASE																																																					
(1)																																																					
(2)																																																					
(3)																																																					
(4)																																																					
(5)																																																					
(6)																																																					

Fig. 83 Annual training plan — blank form.

55

In dividing up the year plan there are four periods which can be included. They are as follows:

General Preparation Period   (1)
Special Preparation Period   (2)
Competition Period   (3)
Transitional Period   (6)

The General Preparation Period is the foundation period on which specific fitness is built at a later date. The aim here is to develop general fitness which will allow the runner to cope with quality specific training in the special preparation period. Included here will be the establishing of a solid base of aerobic endurance as well as the development of local muscular endurance, strength and mobility. This is also the time to develop new techniques or correct faults. Preventative work and therapy for injuries should also be pursued during this period.

Of major importance during this period for all endurance athletes is the laying of a sound aerobic base. A mixture of aerobic training is pursued and over the course of this period the volume or running being undertaken will gradually increase. Towards the end of this period the volume may level out, especially if the runner is intending participating in cross country competition.

The Special Preparation Period builds on the general fitness developed in the general preparation period. New levels of general fitness allow the athlete to develop specific fitness for his main discipline. The aims here are the development of the specific blend of speed and endurance required in the athlete's chosen event. It is also a time to prepare for the technical and tactical demands of the event. At the same time sufficient general training should remain in the training programme to maintain the levels of fitness which were developed in the previous period (the amount of training required to maintain fitness being less than that required to achieve it in the first place).

The aims of the Competition Period will vary according to the athlete's age, status and event. Some athletes might have a simple competition period where the aim is to cut back the training in order that the athlete can achieve his competitive goals. Here the athlete's training load will be reduced significantly allowing the athlete full recovery and one major competitive peak will be pursued.

The competition period may however be divided up into three phases. These would be:

Minor/Qualifying Competition Period   (3)
Competition Preparation Period   (4)
Major/International Competition Period   (5)

In the Minor or Qualifying Period the aim is to progress the runner gradually from relatively unimportant competitions to important events like championships which may qualify him for a team or higher level of competition. This phase is used to develop competitive experience and competition specific fitness.

The Competition (Preparation) Period is a recharging phase in the middle of the competition period which is used to top up specific fitness and prepare for the major competitions. It is also used to correct any technical problems which exist before these major competitions come round.

The Competition (Major/International) Period is the period when training is reduced to encourage maximum recovery and where the runner concentrates on developing speed in order that he can achieve competitive goals.

The final period which falls at the end of the competition period is called the Transitional Period. This is a period of time set aside for the runner to rest after a hard season and to await the start of a new training cycle. It should be a period of rest and regeneration.

Examples of annual training plans are shown in figures 80-82 for three different types of endurance runner, and examples of the type of work pursued in each of the main periods are given in Tables 7-9.

Weekly/Monthly Training Plans

Most runners find it easiest to organise training on a weekly basis. As the majority of runners' lives revolve round a regular weekly pattern, a weekly training cycle seems appropriate. The weekly cycle of training is organised so as to alternate hard and easy days, and to vary different types of training such as anaerobic one day and aerobic the next. Most top runners train twice per day on average.

Improvement results from training as a consequence of the principle of overload. Training stresses or overloads the body forcing it to adapt to the stress and creating an improvement in functional performance. For training to continue to stress the body over a period of time, it needs to be altered on a regular basis. Training should therefore be changed, adjusted or made more demanding every four to eight weeks and for this reason the organisation of training on a monthly basis is recommended. The sample training programmes shown are organised on weekly cycles which last on average four weeks.

After mapping out the annual plan into the four main periods, it is necessary to take each of the periods and to divide it up into manageable periods of time. These could be blocks of about four weeks consisting of four weekly cycles. This done, it is necessary to decide on objectives for the first monthly cycle of training and to format a weekly training plan. The weekly training plan outlines the type of work to be conducted on each day. Once this has been established, the content of each session with its progressions can be inserted and the training schedule for the month produced.

Towards the end of each of the monthly cycles, it will be necessary to review what has been achieved and to decide on what changes will be introduced into the next training schedule.

Sample Training Programmes — 800m runner

Event:	*800m*	Time Period:	*November*
Phase:	*General*	Duration:	*4 weeks*

MON: *Medium paced running & weights*

    AM: 30 mins medium paced running.

    PM: Weights: 1. Power cleans
         Reps 5-8   2. Bench press
                    3. Back squat

        plus 5 sets of abdominal crunch, heel raise and hamstring curl.

        30 mins medium paced running.

TUE: *Easy paced running, technique & speed endurance*
AM: 30 mins easy paced running.
PM: 2 × 4 × 60m with 1 min recovery and 5 mins rest.
Week 1:   5 × 400m (2 mins recovery — 200m jog)
Week 2:   6 × 300m (2 mins recovery — 100m jog)
Week 3:   7 × 250m (2 mins recovery — 150m jog)
Week 4:   8 × 200m (90 secs recovery — 150m jog)

WED: *Easy paced run & fast paced run*
AM: 30 mins easy paced running.
PM: 45 mins fast paced running.

THU: *Medium paced running & weights*
AM: 30 mins medium paced running.
PM: Weights: 1. High Pulls
                          2. Military press
Reps 10-15   3. Arm curls
                          4. Back arm extension

plus 5 sets of abdominal crunch, back raise and straight leg raise.

30 mins medium paced running.

FRI: *Rest day or easy paced run*

SAT: *Elastic strength & interval training off track*
Assorted elastic strength exercises.

5 × 4 mins running on undulating parkland including hills. Must be parkland to ensure good quality of running. Rest of 2 mins.

SUN: *Long aerobic run*
60 mins medium paced running.

Table 7(a): *800m runner: General phase.*

Event:	*800m*	Time Period:	*May*
Phase:	*Special*	Duration:	*4 weeks*

MON: *Medium paced running & weights*
AM: 30 mins medium paced running.
PM: Weights: 1. Power clean
                          2. Bench press
Reps — 5   3. Back squat
plus sets of abdominal crunch, heel raise and hamstring curl.
30 mins medium paced running.

TUE: *Easy paced running, speed & speed endurance*
AM: 30 mins easy paced running.
PM: 2 × 4 × 50m with Walk Back Recovery.
Week 1: 2 × 3 × 200m with WBR and 15 mins rest
Week 2: 4 × 300m (150/150) with 5 mins recovery
Week 3: 400m (5), 300m (5), 200m (20), 4 × 150m
Week 4: 3 × 200m WBR, 15 mins, 4 × 150m WBR.

WED: *Medium paced running & weights*
AM: 30 mins medium paced running.
PM: Weights: 1. High pulls
                  2. Military press
Reps — 12   3. Arm curls
                  4. Back arm extension
plus sets of abdominal crunch, back raise and straight leg raise.
30 mins medium paced running.

THU: *Easy paced running & specific endurance*
AM: 30 mins easy paced running.
PM: Week 1: 2 × 4 × 200m with 30 secs recovery and 20 mins rest.
Week 2: 2 × 200m (30s recovery), 400m (45s), 200m with 20 mins rest.
Week 3: 2 × 2 × 300m with 30 secs recovery and 20 mins rest.
Week 4: 2 × 2 × 400m with 45 secs recovery and 20 mins rest.

FRI: *Rest day or easy paced run*

SAT: *Elastic strength & specific endurance*
3 × 3 × 5 hurdle jumps.
3 × 30m × sprint action touch-off drill.
3 × 20m × bounding.
3 × 30m × straight leg jumps.
Week 1: 1000m, 20 mins rest, 600m.
Week 2: 600m, 20 mins, 400m, 20 mins, 600m.
Week 3: 1000m, 20 mins rest, 600m.
Week 4: 600m/30 secs/200m, 20-30 mins, 600m/30 secs/200m.

SUN: *Long aerobic run*
60 mins medium paced running.

Table 7(b): *800m runner: Special phase.*

Event:	*800m*	Time Period:	*July*
Phase:	*Competition*	Duration:	*4 weeks*

MON: *Medium paced running & weights*
AM: 30 mins medium paced running.
PM: Strength maintenance weights:
    1. Power clean   Reps: 5
    2. Back squat
    3. Bench press
    plus selection of special strength exercises.
    30 mins medium paced running.

TUE: *Easy paced run, elastic strength & specific endurance*
AM: 30 mins easy paced run.
PM: Week 1: 2 × 400m (45s), 200m (30s), 200m with 20 mins plus rest.
    Week 2: 2 × 200m (30s), 400m (45s), 200m with 20 mins plus rest.
    Week 3: 2 × 2 × 300m with 30 secs recovery and 20 mins plus rest.
    Week 4: 2 × 400m (45s), 200m with 20 mins plus rest.
    3 × 3 × 5 hurdle jumps.
    3 × 30m × sprint action touch-off drill.
    3 × 20m × bounding.
    3 × 30m × straight leg jumps.

WED: *Medium paced run*
45 mins of medium paced running.

THU: *Easy paced run, speed & speed endurance*
AM: 30 mins easy paced run.
PM: 2 × 30m, 40m, 50m, 60m with WBR.
    Week 1: 2 × 3 × 200m with WBR and 15 mins rest.
    Week 2: 2 × 4 × 150m with WBR/15 mins.
    Week 3: 4 × 300m (150/150) with 5 mins recovery.
    Week 4: 300m (5), 2 × 200m (5/20), 4 × 150m (WBR).

FRI: *Rest*

SAT: *Competition*

SUN: *Long medium paced run*
45-60 mins medium paced running.

Table 7(c): *800m runner: Competition phase.*

Sample Training Programmes — 5000m runner

Event:	*5000m*	Time Period:	*November*
Phase:	*General*	Duration:	*4 weeks*

MON: *Medium paced running*
 AM: 3 miles medium paced run.
 PM: 6 miles medium paced run.

TUE: *Easy paced running & interval running*
 AM: 3 miles easy paced run.
 PM: 5 × 1 mile runs on grass with 90 secs recovery.

WED: *Medium paced running & circuit training*
 AM: 3 miles medium paced run.
 PM: Circuit training   5 ×

        30 abdominal crunch
        12 straight leg raises
        12 press-ups
        12 back lifts
        12 hamstring curl
         8 arm dips
    5 miles medium paced running.

THU: *Easy paced run & fartlek session*
 AM: 3 miles easy paced running.
 PM: 5 miles fartlek.

FRI: *Easy paced recovery run*
 2-3 miles easy recovery run.

SAT: *Medium paced running*
 AM: 3 miles medium paced run.
 PM: 6 miles medium paced run.

SUN: *Long easy-medium paced run*
 10 miles run at easy-medium pace.

Table 8(a): *5000m runner: General phase.*

Event:	*5000m*	Time Period:	*May*
Phase:	*Special*	Duration:	*4 weeks*

MON: *Medium paced running & stage training*
　　　AM: 3 miles medium paced run.
　　　PM: Stage training　　6 × with 30 secs rest.
　　　　　　　　　　　　　　30 abdominal crunch
　　　　　　　　　　　　　　12 straight leg raises
　　　　　　　　　　　　　　12 press-ups
　　　　　　　　　　　　　　12 back lifts
　　　　　　　　　　　　　　12 hamstring curl
　　　　　　　　　　　　　　8 arm dips
　　　　　　6 miles medium paced run.

TUE: *Easy paced running & specific endurance*
　　　AM: 3 miles easy paced run.
　　　PM: Week 1: 5 × 1000m with 200m recovery.
　　　　　 Week 2: 2 × 3000m with 20 mins recovery.
　　　　　 Week 3: 4 × 1500m with 300m recovery.
　　　　　 Week 4: 4 × 2000m with 5 mins recovery.

WED: *Medium & fast paced running*
　　　AM: 4 miles medium paced run.
　　　PM: 5 miles fast paced running.

THU: *Easy paced run and specific endurance*
　　　AM: 5 miles easy paced running.
　　　PM: Week 1: 12 × 400m with 100m jog recovery.
　　　　　 Week 2: 8 × 600m with 200m jog recovery.
　　　　　 Week 3: 6 × 800m with 200m jog recovery.
　　　　　 Week 4: 10 × 500m with 100m jog recovery.

FRI: *Easy paced recovery run*
　　　2-3 miles easy recovery run.

SAT: *Easy paced running & speed endurance*
　　　AM: 5 miles medium paced run.
　　　PM: Week 1: 2 × 6 × 200m with 200m jog recovery and 15 mins rest.
　　　　　 Week 2: 6 × 500m with 3 mins recovery.
　　　　　 Week 3: 2 × 5 × 300m with 100m jog recovery and 15 mins rest.
　　　　　 Week 4: 2 × 4 × 400m with 200m jog recovery and 15 mins rest.

SUN: *Long medium paced run*
　　　12-15 miles run at medium pace.

Table 8(b): *5000m runner: Special phase.*

Event:	*5000m*	Time Period:	*July*
Phase:	*Competition*	Duration:	*4 weeks*

MON: *Easy paced running & specific endurance*
AM: 4 miles easy paced run.
PM: Week 1: 5 × 1000m with 200m recovery.
Week 2: 12 × 400m with 100m jog recovery.
Week 3: 4 × 1500m with 300m recovery.
Week 4: 8 × 600m with 200m jog recovery.

TUE: *Medium paced running*
AM: 4 miles medium paced run.
PM: 6-8 miles medium paced run.

WED: *Easy paced running and speed endurance*
AM: 4 miles easy paced run.
PM: Week 1: 2 × 5 × 300m with 100m jog recovery and 20 mins rest.
Week 2: 2 × 4 × 400m with 100m jog recovery and 20 mins rest.
Week 3: 2 × 3 × 500m with 100m jog recovery and 20 mins rest.
Week 4: 2 × 6 × 200m with 100m jog recovery and 20 mins rest.

THU: *Easy paced running*
AM: 4 miles easy paced running.
PM: 5-6 miles easy paced running.

FRI: *Easy paced recovery run*
2-3 miles easy recovery run.

SAT: *Competition*

SUN: *Long medium paced run*
10 miles run at medium pace.

Table 8(c): *5000m runner: Competition phase.*

Sample Training Programmes — Marathon runner

Event:	*Marathon*		
Phase:	*General*	Duration:	*4 weeks*

MON: *Medium paced running*
  AM: 3 miles medium paced run.
  PM: 6 miles medium paced run.

TUE: *Easy paced running & interval running*
  AM: 3 miles easy paced run.
  PM: 5 × 1 mile interval runs with 2 mins recovery.

WED: *Medium paced running & circuit training*
  AM: 3 miles medium paced run.
  PM: Circuit training   5 ×

                    30 abdominal crunch
                    12 straight leg raises
                    12 press-ups
                    12 back lifts
                    12 hamstring curl
                     8 arm dips
       5 miles medium paced running.

THU: *Easy paced run and fartlek session*
  AM: 3 miles easy paced running.
  PM: 5 miles fartlek.

FRI: *Easy paced recovery run*
  2-3 miles easy recovery run.

SAT: *Medium paced running*
  AM: 3 miles medium paced run.
  PM: 6 miles medium paced run.

SUN: *Long easy-medium paced run*
  10 miles run at easy-medium pace.

Table 9(a): *Marathon runner: General phase.*

Event:	Marathon		
Phase:	Special	Duration:	4 weeks

MON: *Easy and medium paced running*
AM: 3-4 miles easy paced run.
PM: 6-8 miles medium paced run.

TUE: *Easy paced & interval running*
AM: 3-4 miles easy paced run.
PM: 5 × 1 mile interval runs with 2 mins recovery.

WED: *Easy and medium paced running*
AM: 3-4 miles easy paced run.
PM: 6-8 miles medium paced run.

THU: *Easy paced run and fast run*
AM: 3 miles easy paced running.
PM: 10 miles fast paced run.

FRI: *Easy paced recovery run*
2-3 miles easy recovery run.

SAT: *Medium paced run*
AM: 3-4 miles medium paced run.
PM: 10 miles medium paced run.

SUN: *Long run*
Week 1: 20 miles.
Week 2: 12-15 miles.
Week 3: 20 miles.
Week 4: 12-15 miles.

Table 9(b): *Marathon runner: Special phase.*

Event:	*Marathon*		
Phase:	*Competition Taper*	Duration:	*2 weeks*

SUN: Long run of 15 miles duration

MON: 4 miles easy running

TUE: AM: 4 miles easy running.
PM: 8 miles medium paced run.

WED: 6 miles easy running

THU: AM: 3 miles easy running.
PM: 8 miles at medium pace.

FRI: 5 miles medium paced running

SAT: 5 × 1 mile interval running with 2 mins recovery

SUN: 10 mile run at marathon pace

MON: 5 miles medium paced running

TUE: 5 miles medium paced running

WED: 3-4 miles easy running

THU: 3-4 miles easy running

FRI: 3-4 miles easy running

SAT: Race day

Table 9(c): *Marathon runner: Competition Taper phase.*

CHAPTER 6
COMPETITION STRATEGIES

A Measure of Success

Success in a race can be measured in a number of different ways, not just in terms of who won and who lost. Although every athlete who lines up on the starting line of a race would like to be the winner, the reality is that only one person can win. This does not mean that the other competitors will not experience their own personal success. Each athlete is able to set a number of goals for each race in which he participates. As there can only be one winner in a race, it is likely that not all competitors set winning as their main goal. Some will be realistic and assess their chances of being first as being minimal. They will enter the race with other objectives such as improving their placing in the race relative to their ranking. The sixth ranked runner might for example be trying to place in the first three or to run a personal best time, both realistic goals for an athlete who finds himself in a fast field.

Whatever the level of competition, it is necessary for each competitor to establish goals or targets for each of his/her races. In doing so the runner is taking positive steps to make the likelihood of success more possible and to minimise the possibility of failure.

The goals that an athlete sets for a particular race should possess the following features:

— they should be challenging and have a degree of difficulty that requires the runner to raise his effort to achieve them.

— they should be agreed between the athlete and coach and they should be unrestricted.

— multiple goals which increase the likelihood of a positive outcome should be set and prioritised. Multiple goals might include the runner's finishing position, finishing time, or just accomplishing an agreed strategy, etc.

— they should be capable of being observed and measured. For example, having a ''good run'' is a matter of personal opinion whilst running the first lap in 55 secs can be timed and therefore measured.

— they should have a high probability of being achieved. The runner must be capable, even if it does require an extra special effort, of achieving the set task.

— they should only contain items that can be controlled by the athlete.

— they should be stated positively.

— they should be believed by the athlete.

The competition strategy adopted by the runner and the tactics to be employed in implementing that strategy will be determined to a large extent by the goals the runner sets for the competition.

Competition Strategies

The runner's strategy and choice of tactics are determined by the goals set, the runner's strengths and weaknesses, the qualities of the opposition and the nature of the race.

If our runner is well conditioned and has good sprinting speed, it may be possible that he/she can adjust to whatever tactics are employed. On the other hand if our runner is lacking endurance but is blessed with good speed, he/she may wish to dictate a slow early pace in the hope of using a superior sprint finish in the home straight. A third possibility would be that the runner has good endurance but lacks speed and, in this case, will want either to front run the race or employ an extended sprint for the finish line.

The runner also has to consider the opposition and will need to know whether they are of a similar ability level or are much faster or slower. Knowledge of how they prefer to race, their ability to sprint finish and their levels of conditioning will help our runner decide how to tackle the race.

The type of race will also determine how it is approached. A major race, for example, will produce committed performances from all competitors. A minor race however will lead to experimentation and it may not be treated with the same importance by all competitors. The race may be one of a sequence such as a series of qualifying heats, semi-finals and finals, requiring each race to be considered in the context of the other races in the series.

Consideration of these three factors, the runner's strengths and weaknesses, the qualities of the opposition and the type of race will lead to decisions being made regarding how our runner will approach the race. The runner's racing plan or strategy should be agreed by the runner and the coach and may be written down using a competition strategy sheet similar to that shown in Table 10.

The competition strategy has two components, the first being the runner's preferred racing plan, the actions he/she wishes to take to run the race his/her way. The race is divided up into a number of segments and tasks are set for each. Dividing up the race into a number of segments allows the runner to concentrate on a number of intermediate goals on the way to achieving the overall goal for the race. By concentrating on the successful accomplishment of these intermediate tasks a positive task oriented approach to competition is achieved, giving no opportunity for losses of concentration or confidence.

It is rare however when everything goes to plan, so it is necessary for the runner to develop a secondary strategy to deal with unexpected changes to the way the race is run. The secondary or coping strategy provides options for the runner to take in the event of such changes to race pattern. Even though there are a number of different scenarios possible in a race, only one secondary strategy needs to be planned. The process of considering an alternative strategy sensitizes the runner to the need to make quick decisions when the race does not go to plan and helps him/her cope with these changes. An example of a racing strategy is shown in Table 10. It should be noted that these strategies only include positive actions and positive self statements.

Tactical Considerations

One of the most successful tactics in endurance running is to run on the shoulder of the leader(s) in order that you can cover your opposition's moves, and to gather yourself for a strong finish over the finishing stages of the race.

The fast finisher may in some races wish to take the lead early to slow down a fast pace in order that he can use his superior finish.

If the runner is not confident in his ability to out-sprint the opposition, he may wish to dull the sprint finish of his rivals by taking the lead early and dictating a fast even pace throughout the race or even increasing the pace

COMPETITION STRATEGY FORM

NAME: ANNE ATHLETE	EVENT: 1500m FINAL	VENUE: C.P.	DATE: 17·07·87

RACE PLAN	COPING STRATEGY	EVALUATION
EXPECT GOOD PACE OF AROUND 4.10.00 I.E. 67│2.14│3.21│4.10. **1ST 300m** STEADY START, LET OTHERS TAKE UP LEAD POSITIONS. SETTLE AT BACK FOR FIRST 200m & THEN WORK THROUGH GRADUALLY TO COVER LEADERS. TRY TO STAY ON OUTSIDE BUT IN 1ST LANE. **300m – 1000m** HOLD POSITION, DO NOT LET RUNNERS MOVE ROUND & BOX IN. KEEP WATCH ON LEADERS **1000m – 1500m** BE READY TO TAKE INITIATIVE FROM 500m OUT. IF I SENSE THAT SOMEONE IS ABOUT TO KICK, I WILL KICK 1ST & RUN FOR HOME. IF NO-ONE MOVES BY 250m TO GO, I WILL KICK HERE AND RUN FOR HOME. WHEN I START FINISH RUN, I WILL CONCENTRATE ON FORM, WILL LOOK AHEAD & WILL RUN THROUGH LINE.	IF PACE IS SLOW, HOLD BACK & AVOID BECOMING BOXED IN. IF FAST, STICK TO PLAN AS I HAVE STRENGTH TO KICK OFF GOOD PACE. IF BOXED IN, DO NOT PANIC, WAIT FOR GAP AND MOVE OUT GENTLY. IF SOMEONE DOES GET AWAY FROM ME, I WILL NOT PANIC BUT WILL CONTINUE TO RUN FOR HOME. THIS MAY PLACE ME OR BRING GOOD TIME.	RACE WENT TO PLAN. LOST SOME FORM IN HOME STRAIGHT. MUST WORK ON MAINTAINING GOOD SPRINTING FORM WHEN FATIGUED. TIME: 4.11.47

Table 10: *Competition strategy form — example.*

gradually section by section.

Another possibility is to throw in a fast section in a race with the same aim in mind of knocking out the opposition's kick. An example would be to throw in a fast third 400m in a 1500m.

If the athlete has good speed endurance but lacks the ability to accelerate, he could choose to make a run for home from further out than 150m, perhaps from 300m or 400m or 500m. Some athletes have even made a run for home from as far out as 1000m or, in the case of the marathon, in the closing miles of the race.

The ability to employ tactics on the track such as the:

— sprint finish over last 200m,
— extended sprint finish over distances up to 1000m,
— fast lap in the middle of the race,
— running the second half of the race at a faster pace than the first,
— running gradually faster sections,
— front running a fast even pace,

can be developed during specific endurance sessions by arranging training sessions to simulate these conditions.

In the marathon tactics such as front running, even paced running or a fast finish somewhere in the last 10,000m need to be considered on the basis of the athlete's level of conditioning and basic running speed.

If a runner wishes to dictate the pace of a race he/she will have to run at the front of the field. This has a disadvantage in that the runner may not be able to see what the opposition are doing, whilst they can observe all of his/her moves. The runner wishing to cover all possible moves in a race is best placed running on the shoulder of the leader(s). Here the runner can cover moves by the front runners and by those who might come from behind. A watch must be kept for several runners coming round the runner at once and forcing him/her back into a "boxed-in" position where he/she can no longer cover moves as the route forward is blocked.

The runner who becomes boxed in should not panic, but rather wait for an opening to develop. It is also possible to create an opening by gradually moving out, forcing the runners on the outside shoulder to move wide. Care should be taken however not to interfere with the opposition as this could lead to disqualification.

Running at the back of the field, especially at the start, can keep the runner clear of any bumping, barging or boxing that may occur. However, the runner needs the confidence that he/she is fit enough to do this and still be able to progress through the field towards the front later in the race.

In track races it is best to run as close to the inside of the track as possible as this represents the shortest distance. Running wide can add a few metres to the length of your race. You may however need to run slightly wide to cover the leader(s). On a windy day, the runner should try to tuck in behind another competitor, in order to reduce effort. When passing the opposition, especially if the runner is committed to running for home, this should be done with conviction. The opposition should not be given time to react and cover the move. Take them by surprise and they may never catch you. Passing on the straight is easier than passing on the bend. This is especially true on an indoor 200m track. As a rule you will pass on the outside, but often in races a gap appears on the inside of the track which allows a shorter route. When taking the inside route, care be taken to ensure that the other runners are not interfered with.

An important consideration in steeplechasing is the 28 hurdles and 7 water jumps. Effective clearance of these barriers to a large extent is determined by the runner's ability to pick them out as he approaches. This requires the steeplechaser to position himself so that he has a clear view and at the same time make decisions on how to race the other competitors.

It is advisable when racing to avoid looking back. Runners have often been caught looking over one shoulder, relaxing and not seeing a runner coming through on the other side. It can also be viewed by the opposition as a sign that you are weakening and give them encouragement to raise their effort.

When leading out of the final bend, accelerate into the straight to stay ahead. As you come off a bend drift slightly towards the outside of the inside lane.

In tournament conditions, with heats and qualifying rounds, thought needs to be given to the best approach to competing in a number of races. The aim in heats is to qualify for the final with the minimum of effort. The runner must remain alert though for unexpected moves, and take care to make sure that he/she is not run out by being too casual. There is also an argument for runners winning qualifying rounds, as this gives the athlete a positive feeling for the next round or final. A strong competitor also has the chance of making each subsequent round harder in order to fatigue those athletes with a known fast finish.

Concentration

Concentrating and staying alert during a race is a key factor in determining success. The runner who loses concentration will fail to respond when the opposition makes a break and may never get back into the race. Loss of concentration may result in the runner failing to run the race to the best of his ability. Concentration has to be practised in training, in particular in specific endurance training sessions. The use of a competition strategy will enhance concentration by enabling the runner to focus prior to and during the race on the tasks to be performed and by encouraging the runner to adopt a positive approach.

Confidence

A runner's confidence can be boosted by the use of goal setting and competition strategies. The use of effective goal setting should see the majority of runners achieving the majority of their goals provided those goals have remained achievable. Competition strategies involve a positive task oriented approach to competition features compatible with increased confidence.

Race Pace

In running 800m the pace of the first and second laps are often considered as a guide to racing pace. Consideration of these factors may be most relevant when trying to achieve a personal best time. It is said that the first lap can safely be run 4 secs slower than your best 400m time. This means an athlete with a best of 50 secs for the 400m could run a first lap of 54 with comfort. It is also said that the ideal differential between the first and second laps of an 800m is 2.5 secs. This would mean that the second lap could be run in 56.5 secs giving a total time for the 800m of 1:50.5.

Of course not all races are run at this so-called ideal pace, with the first lap being slightly faster than the second. Some races feature a faster second lap and others two even-paced laps.

It is said that the first 800m of a 1500m should be run 8 secs slower than your best time for 800m and that the 1500m is best run at even pace. This would mean an athlete with a best for 800m of 2:08.00 would run the laps of a 1500m at 68 secs pace leading to a time of 4:15.00.

Pace in the 3000m steeplechase when aiming to run a good time should be even, but this is difficult to establish with different sizes of track. The following table indicates even pace for an 8:30.00 run on two different types of track.

Track with water jump inside track

Distance from start to finish line:	242m	41.14 secs
Distance of each full lap:	394m	66.98 secs

Track with water jump outside track on an eight-lane track

Distance from start to finish line:	60m	10.2 secs
Distance of each full lap:	420m	71.4 secs

Tables 3, 4 and 5 on pages 19, 22 and 23 are useful guides to even pace running for long distance and marathon events.

CHAPTER 7

PHYSIOLOGY OF ENDURANCE RUNNING

Success in endurance running is dependent on the runner being able to sustain his running speed over a period of time. The development of this unique combination of both speed and endurance is the priority in training. The faster an athlete runs, the greater the quantity of energy that has to be delivered to the working muscles. In this section we examine how the energy systems deliver energy to the muscles, what limits them and how they adapt in order to make more energy available.

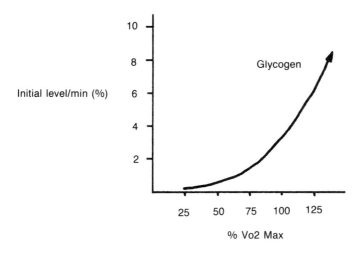

Fig. 84 Energy demands with increasing intensity of activity. (Adapted from Brotherhood.)

The major muscles of the arms and legs are involved in the running action, contracting and relaxing in order to propel the body forwards. Within these major muscles are muscle fibres so thin that they cannot be seen by the human eye, and which run the whole length of the muscle. These fibres are recruited to shorten in order to contract the muscles, and then return to their normal length when the muscle relaxes. Each time a muscle fibre shortens it uses energy which comes in the form of a substance called adenosine triphosphate (ATP).

Three Energy Systems

Adenosine triphosphate (ATP), the energy source that our muscles need, is a molecule consisting of an atom of adenosine surrounded by three phosphate atoms. When the muscle fibres shorten along their lengths, ATP is used and as a result one of the phosphate atoms is lost, changing the ATP into another substance called adenosine diphosphate (ADP).

$$A - P \xrightarrow[\text{"muscle contraction"}]{} A - P + P$$

Without ATP the muscle fibres cannot shorten and movement cannot occur. If an athlete is to be able to run, his muscles need a constant supply of ATP. The aim of endurance training is to ensure that our muscles have an adequate supply of energy in the form of ATP and to enable them to use that energy.

Energy in the form of ATP is provided through one of the following three energy systems:

1. Alactic — Anaerobic Energy System.
   (Phosphate stores; no lactic acid produced; no oxygen required.)
2. Lactic — Anaerobic Energy System.
   (Carbohydrate as fuel; lactic acid produced; no oxygen required.)
3. Aerobic Energy System.
   (Carbohydrate and fats as fuel; no lactic acid produced; oxygen present.)

Alactic Anaerobic System

There is a small store of ATP contained within our muscles which would last for around four seconds if we exercised as hard as we could. Any exercise which lasts for more than four seconds requires fresh ATP to be found from one of the three energy systems. The most immediate source of new ATP is found within the muscles' stores of another phosphate called creatine phosphate (CP). The ADP created when an ATP loses one of its phosphates combines with the CP to re-convert itself to ATP. It does this by borrowing the CP's phosphate.

$$A - P + C - P \xrightarrow{\hspace{3cm}} A - P + C$$

This method of producing ATP is also short term, as the muscles' stores of creatine phosphate are limited — only three to four times the size of the ATP stores and therefore lasting around twelve seconds.

To produce more ATP, the muscles will now have to break down one of two fuel sources available in the body, either carbohydrate or fats. Carbohydrate can be broken down to produce ATP either in the presence of oxygen, referred to as aerobic metabolism (aerobic means with oxygen), or without oxygen present, referred to as anaerobic metabolism (anaerobic means without oxygen). Fats on the other hand can only be broken down by the aerobic process.

Aerobic System

Provided there is an adequate supply of oxygen to the working muscles, carbohydrate in the form of muscle glycogen and fats in the form of free fatty acids can be metabolised to produce ATP. With the encouragement of oxidative enzymes (organic catalysts which release and transfer energy) these two fuels are reduced to carbon dioxide and water. In the process they produce a number of ATP molecules.

Carbohydrate, available in the muscles as glycogen, is first of all converted to pyruvic acid in a process known as glycolysis, producing three ATP molecules. The pyruvic acid is then taken up by cells within the muscles called mitochondria. The oxygen in the muscles is also taken up by these cells, which are often referred to as the 'engine rooms' of the muscle. In the mitochondria, the pyruvic acid and oxygen are converted to carbon dioxide and water in a process which produces 36 ATP molecules. The total number of ATP produced by the aerobic metabolism of a unit of carbohydrate is 39.

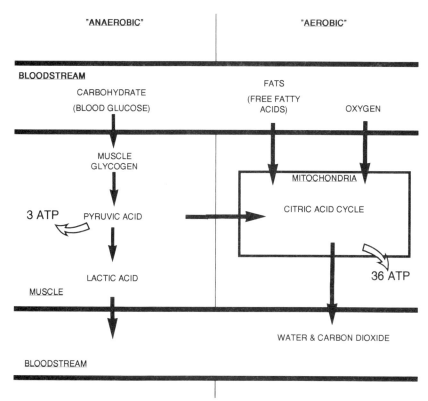

Fig. 85 Aerobic and anaerobic production of ATP.

Fats are available in the muscle as free fatty acids and they too, like the pyruvic acid, can be taken up by the mitochondria. Just as the pyruvic acid combines with the oxygen to produce 36 ATP, so do the free fatty acids. The oxidation of fats produces 36 ATP as opposed to 39 produced when the fuel is carbohydrate. This explains why 12% more oxygen is used to produce the same amount of energy from fats as from carbohydrates. Although fats are not as rich an energy source as carbohydrates, they have the advantage of being an almost inexhaustible store when compared to that of carbohydrate, which is only large enough to supply energy for approximately 100 minutes of continuous steady state running.

Free fatty acids are an important source of energy for long distance running events, such as the marathon, where it is necessary to mobilise fats stores in order to spread the use of carbohydrate over the duration of the event. The average runner uses about 50% carbohydrate and 50% fats when running at marathon pace. Through training, the percentage of fats used can be increased.

The relatively short duration and high speeds of events from 800m through to 10,000m places high demands for energy which are best met by using carbohydrates as the main source of energy.

Lactic Anaerobic Energy

When there is insufficient oxygen available in the muscle to meet all of the energy demands through the aerobic system, energy can be made available through the anaerobic metabolism of carbohydrate. The muscle glycogen is converted into pyruvic acid by glycolysis (described above). As there is no oxygen available to combine with the pyruvic acid, there is no point in it being taken up by the mitochondria. The pyruvic acid is therefore converted to lactic acid. Unlike the waste products of aerobic metabolism which are easily dispersed, lactic acid has to wait until oxygen becomes available at a later stage to allow it to be re-converted to pyruvate or even glycogen. Until that happens, the lactic acid which accumulates in the muscle and spills over into the bloodstream has a negative influence on performance.

The lactic acid which remains within the muscle inhibits the enzymes which enable glycogen to be converted to energy anaerobically and also inhibits the muscles from contracting. If too much lactate is allowed to build up in the muscles, the athlete will eventually be forced to cease running or at least to slow down. From this viewpoint the production of lactic acid may be considered a negative limiting factor. However, in middle distance events large amounts of energy need to be made available quickly to allow these distances to be run at speed. Although the anaerobic conversion of carbohydrate does not yield much energy for each unit used, the rate at which energy is released far exceeds the speed of energy production from the aerobic energy process. From this viewpoint the production of lactic acid enhances performance in endurance events.

The Key Systems

The proportion of energy contributed by each of the three energy systems is related to the speed of running. The faster an athlete runs, the greater the energy required (see Figure 84).

When a runner sprints over 100m he requires a large amount of energy to be delivered to his muscles in a relatively short space of time. The alactic anaerobic energy system can provide energy quickly in relatively large amounts, but the store is exhausted in a few seconds. The person running over 800m also needs a lot of energy quickly — not at as high a rate as the 100m runner, but certainly at a higher rate than can be delivered by the aerobic system alone. As energy from the alactic anaerobic system is depleted quickly, the 800m runner has to rely on the lactic anaerobic energy system as the major contributor of energy. The longer the event the slower the pace, and the greater the contribution by the aerobic system.

In endurance running events the key contributors of energy are the aerobic and lactic anaerobic systems. Whilst the alactic anaerobic system does supply some energy in the course of these events its contribution is small. The estimated contribution of the aerobic and anaerobic systems to the energy requirements of the endurance running events are shown below:

Event	Aerobic	Anaerobic
800m	35%	65%
1500m	50%	50%
3000m	60%	40%
3000m S/C	70%	30%
5000m	80%	20%
10,000m	90%	10%
Marathon	95%	5%

Table 11: *Aerobic and Anaerobic Systems' Contribution to Energy Demands in Endurance Running Events.*

The three energy systems should not be thought of as operating independently of each other. It is not a case of one system being recruited as the other becomes exhausted. The three systems are constantly making some contribution to the body's energy requirements.

Aerobic Capacity

A well developed aerobic system is essential for success in all endurance running events. Although the contribution of this system to the production of energy increases with the distance being run, a well developed aerobic system in shorter events such as the 800m will assist performance by holding back the use of the anaerobic system.

If energy is to be provided by the aerobic system, a constant supply of oxygen has to be made available to the mitochondria. This oxygen will come from the air that is breathed into the runner's lungs. Air passes down the windpipe and branches into the two moist bags which form the left and right lungs. The two branches which continue to divide into smaller and smaller branches eventually lead to tiny thin walled sacs called alveoli. The total surface area of the thin walls of the alveoli in athletes is greater than $60m^2$. These sacs are surrounded by fine blood vessels called capillaries. The vast area of contact between the bloodstream and the air through the thin walls of the alveoli allows for the efficient transfer of oxygen through the membrane into the bloodstream. As oxygen passes into the blood, carbon dioxide is passed out of the bloodstream into the lungs for expiration. At rest we breathe about twelve times per minute; when running the breathing rate increases to take more air into the lungs.

The blood passing by the thin walls of the lungs in the pulmonary (lung) capillaries is being driven by the pumping action of the heart. The heart is divided into two halves, which are separated by a thick muscular wall. Each side of the heart has two chambers; the upper chamber is called the atrium and the lower the ventricle. There is a valve between the atrium and the ventricle which allows blood to pass in one direction only. Blood which has been circulating around the body's general or systemic circulatory system enters the heart through the right atrium depleted of oxygen. The blood in the right atrium is pumped by the heart into the right ventricle. It is then in turn pumped out of the right ventricle and round the pulmonary circulatory system which

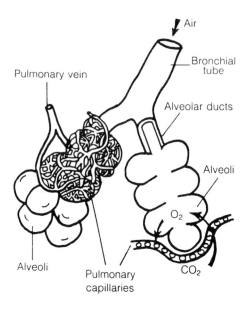

Fig. 86 Oxygen passes from the alveoli into the bloodstream.

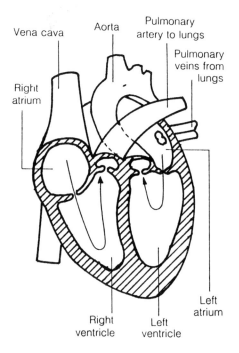

Fig. 87 The heart.

78

passes over the lungs. As the blood passes the lungs it can off-load carbon dioxide and take up oxygen. The blood then continues back to the heart, this time entering the left atrium. The re-oxygenated blood then passes through the valve into the left ventricle before being pumped round the body's systemic circulatory system.

The greater the volume of blood that can be passed round the body's systemic circulation, the more oxygen that can be made available to the muscles. The amount of blood being pumped round the body each minute is determined by the heart's output which is called the *cardiac output*. Cardiac output is the volume of blood being pumped out of the heart per minute. It is calculated by multiplying the volume of blood being expelled during one contraction by the number of times the heart contracts in a minute.

Cardiac Output = Stroke Volume × Heart Rate

Being a muscle, the heart can be trained, making it stronger and capable of increasing the amount of blood that it can squeeze out as it contracts. As a result of this increase in the heart's stroke volume, the rate at which the heart beats at rest or during set workloads decreases. A greater amount of blood can be circulated at a set heart rate supplying more oxygen to the body. As the oxygen required by the body at rest or during a set workload does not increase, the heart does not need to beat as often to supply the oxygen required; hence the heart rate at rest or at a set workload falls as a result of training the heart.

The oxygen which passes into the bloodstream in the lungs is carried by haemoglobin which is contained within the red blood cells. The concentration of haemoglobin in the blood normally ranges between 14.0gm and 16.0gm per 100ml of blood for men and between 12.0gm and 14.0gm per 100ml of blood for women.

As the blood vessels arrive at the working muscles, they branch into a network of fine capillaries which diffuse through the muscle. As the blood containing the red blood cells with their oxygen-carrying haemoglobin molecules passes through the muscle, the oxygen is attracted into the muscle by molecules of a substance called myoglobin. As the oxygen's attraction to myglobin is greater than its attraction to haemoglobin, the oxygen passes from the bloodstream into the muscle. The oxygen attracted from the bloodstream is then used in the mitochondria to oxidise fuel. The waste product of this process, carbon dioxide, is taken up by the blood stream and is transported back via the heart to the lungs where it can be expired.

Maximal Oxygen Uptake

There is a limit to the amount of oxygen that can be transported to and utilised by the muscles. The amount of oxygen used can be determined with specialised equipment which measures the amount of oxygen breathed in and compares this with the amount breathed out. The difference between the two is the amount of oxygen that has been used, and this is referred to as the oxygen uptake. The maximum amount of oxygen that can be utilised by the body is the runner's maximum oxygen uptake (Vo2 Max).

A runner's Vo2 Max is measured in the first instance as the maximum amount of oxygen that is used in one minute, and this will be expressed in litres of oxygen. One runner, for example, may be capable of using 3.5 litres of oxygen per minute. To allow comparisons to be made between different runners, this absolute value is divided by the runner's body weight to give a relative score expressed in millilitres per kilogram of bodyweight per minute (ml/kg/min).

This measure is commonly used to assess levels of aerobic fitness and predict endurance performance. It is an important measure for all endurance runners as success in endurance events is to a large extent dependent on the athlete possessing a high Vo2 Max. The average score for the general population aged 20 to 29 years is 44-51 ml/kg/min for men and 35-43 ml/kg/min for women. Top endurance athletes of a similar age would expect Vo2 Max scores of 70-85 ml/kg/min for men and 65-80 ml/kg/min for women.

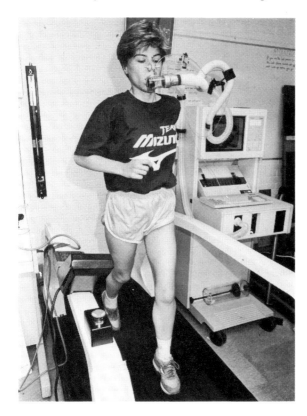

Fig. 88 Vo2 Max being measured in the laboratory.

Anaerobic Threshold

As was explained earlier, the three energy systems work together so at any one time all three are providing energy to working muscles. In training runners, we tend to focus on the energy system which is providing most of our energy requirements. The system that is dominant will vary according to the speed at which the athlete is running, the strength required to maintain that speed, the coordination demands, the duration of sustaining that speed and the involvement of accelerations and decelerations. The transition from the aerobic to anaerobic energy systems as the major source of energy is not, as you might expect, a gradual transition but rather one that is quite marked.

As the intensity or speed of a run increases, the amount of lactic acid being produced as a consequence of the anaerobic energy system being used gradually increases to a certain point. At that point the lactic acid being produced increases dramatically as the anaerobic energy system is rapidly recruited. This is shown in the diagram below. The point at which the production of lactic acid starts to increase rapidly is referred to as the anaerobic threshold, or sometimes as the onset of blood lactic acid (OBLA). A runner's anaerobic threshold can be expressed as a percentage of the runner's Vo2 Max by noting his oxygen uptake at the point where a rapid increase in blood lactate concentration occurs.

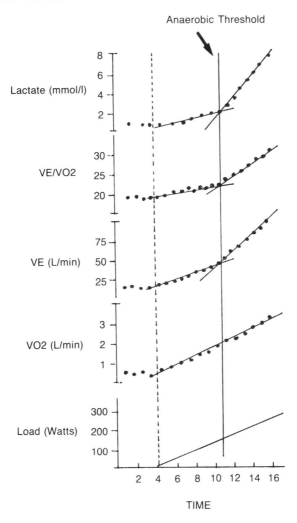

Fig. 89 Physiological test results indicate the anaerobic threshold. (Adapted from Costill.)

In the untrained person the anaerobic threshold would occur at about 50% of his Vo2 Max. Top athletes, on the other hand, would be more efficient and might not reach their anaerobic threshold until tapping as much as 80% of their Vo2 Max.

In Figure 89 the anaerobic threshold can be easily identified by the point at which lactic acid levels in the blood rapidly rise. This point corresponds to a similar rise in ventilation rate (VE). This sudden increase in breathing rate can easily be recognised by athletes running. When running at an easy pace using a percentage of your Vo2 Max below the anaerobic threshold, breathing rates are steady and it is possible to conduct a conversation. When the anaerobic threshold is reached and breathing rates increase rapidly, it is no longer possible to converse without a degree of discomfort. The point where conversation becomes difficult is often used by runners to gauge how hard they are running, and to give a guide to whether they are above or below the anaerobic threshold. This method is called the conversational index. The increase in ventilation rate occurs as a consequence of the increase in lactic acid in the bloodstream. The bloods buffers, in particular bicarbonate, react with the lactic acid to produce carbon dioxide, which is a potent stimulator of respiration.

Lactic Anaerobic Capacity

The normal amount of lactic acid circulating in the bloodstream varies from one individual to another, but is about 1-2 mmol/L (millimoles of lactic per litre of blood). Initially, when you start running this reduces as some lactate is re-converted to pyruvate to produce energy (see Figure 89). In steady state running at relatively slow speeds, blood lactate levels may rise by 1.5-2 times resting levels to about 4 mmol/L, a figure that corresponds to the anaerobic threshold. In faster runs considerably more lactic acid will be produced, as much as 25 mmol/L in well trained athletes undertaking full effort runs of 45 secs to 2 mins. This would be a 15-20 fold increase over resting levels.

The optimal stimulus for steady state running is thought to be about 4 mmol/L, the anaerobic threshold, although this might range in individuals from 2-7.5 mmol/L. This would be the highest intensity of exercise that could be maintained over an extended period of time without a progressive increase in lactic acid concentration occurring.

Lactic acid can be measured by medical staff using simple ear or finger prick samples and a rapid automated lactate analyser. These can be operated at trackside, allowing a testing service to monitor and control aerobic and anaerobic training sessions. This equipment is easy to use and extremely reliable, but it should only be used by trained medical staff.

Training Adaptations

Through training the runner hopes to promote a number of physiological adaptations that will enable him to produce more energy, both aerobically and anaerobically. Adaptations to aerobic training will lead to an improved ability to transport oxygen to the working muscle, and to the muscle's ability to produce energy through oxidation. These will be reflected in an increased maximum oxygen uptake and an improved efficiency indicated by either a higher anaerobic threshold or improved running economy. Adaptations to anaerobic training will lead to an improved capacity to produce energy

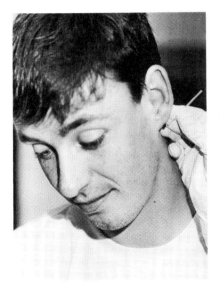

Fig. 90 Blood lactate being taken and analysed.

anaerobically and to tolerate higher levels of lactic acid, both of which are evidenced by higher measures of blood lactate levels.

Aerobic Adaptations

Aerobic training will improve cardiac output through strengthening of the heart muscle allowing it to pump more blood with each beat. This will lead to an observable decrease in resting heart rate values, and to heart rate values for standard training sessions. The total volume of blood in the body increases as a result of training and the blood becomes less viscous, allowing it to flow more easily. The number of red blood cells increases, as does the total amount of haemoglobin in the body. Despite the increase in the total amount of haemoglobin in the body, haemoglobin concentrations may fall as a consequence of the increased blood volume. This sometimes leads to runners incorrectly being diagnosed as being anaemic, when in fact they have increased amounts of haemoglobin in their blood.

The small blood vessels called capillaries, which distribute blood through the working muscles, increase in number due to training. This provides more blood to the muscles, allowing greater amounts of oxygen to be extracted. The myoglobin molecules which attract the oxygen into the muscles from the blood increase in number with training. The mitochondria also increase in number as well as in size. There is also an increase in the concentrations of oxidative enzymes. These adaptations at a muscular level make it possible for more fuel to be converted to energy aerobically.

Lactic Anaerobic Adaptations

Anaerobic training increases anaerobic enzyme activity and the lactic acid buffers of bicarbonate and blood proteins. It also increases the muscles' ability

83

to "pump out" lactic acid into the bloodstream. Training which causes lactic acid levels of about five times resting values will promote lactic anaerobic adaptation. As high lactate levels detract from the quality of training, sufficient recovery has to be allowed in training to allow lactate levels to fall to about the 4-6 mmol/L level. With maximal efforts it would appear that it is necessary to allow at least 20 minutes for this to happen. The recovery period, however, depends on the intensity of the exercise bouts and on how much lactate has been accumulated.

An active recovery will reduce the lactate levels more quickly than a passive recovery. Light aerobic activity causes the lactic acid to be converted back to pyruvate and to be used as a fuel to provide energy for the activity. This has lead to the concept of warming down at the end of training with some light aerobic exercise, the aim being to accelerate the recovery process. There is, however, a body of opinion that rejects warming down in order to oblige the system to build up the lactic acid buffers.

Specificity in Training

At muscular level adaptations to training are highly specific. This means that training has to replicate speeds required in racing in order that the muscle fibres recruited and trained are the same as will be used in competition. The muscle fibres recruited in long steady state runs are predominantly slow twitch or red oxidative fibres. In sprinting they will be fast twitch or white glycolytic fibres. Endurance runners will recruit their own unique combination of different fibres during competition, so steps must be taken to ensure that these are also utilised in training.

Adaptation to New Environments

Runners often find themselves faced with unique physiological demands created by a new environment, such as when they compete in a hot, humid climate or go training at altitude.

Hot environments can produce a range of problems for the runner, from reduced endurance capacity due to dehydration to life threatening heat stroke. Running increases energy production within the body producing heat which has to be lost to the external environment. This is not a problem in our temperate climate where heat is lost easily, but it is in hot climates for runners who have not adapted to the increased heat.

Heat generated in the runner's muscles is transferred out towards the body surface. Excess body heat is lost through convection (air passing over the skin), radiation (heat taken up by cooler air), and conduction (heat taken up by cooler objects). It is also lost through our expired air and through evaporation of sweat from the skin.

In a hot environment, body heat might be lost by convection if there is a wind blowing or by air passing over the athlete as he runs. Radiation and conduction are poor sources of heat loss in warm climates as the air and objects in the environment are warm. If the external temperature rises to more than 33-34°C (92°F), radiation and conduction will work in reverse, heating the body instead of cooling it. The body may also absorb heat radiating from the sun and this may add further to the problem of losing heat generated by the exercise.

Loss of heat through expired air is also inefficient in a hot climate. When it is cold, heat is lost through the water vapour in the exhaled breath. This is observed when it is extremely cold by the mist that occurs as you breathe out. We also tend to breathe on to our hands when it is cold to warm them up. In a hot environment, however, very little heat is lost this way.

In a warm climate most body heat will be lost through the evaporation of sweat from the skin. This is easiest in a hot dry climate, and more difficult in a hot humid climate where the air, heavily saturated with moisture, stops the sweat from being evaporated off the skin. The inability to get rid of the sweat in hot humid environments can cause runners to overheat.

Sweating itself leads to loss of body fluid which, if excessive, could reduce endurance capacity. A 2-3% weight loss, for example, could lead to a 7-8% reduction in endurance capacity. Body fluid needs to be replaced through drinking so as to avoid dehydration, a major source of problems for our endurance runners when they compete abroad in hot environments.

It is necessary when travelling to a hot country to ensure an adequate intake of water by regular drinking which can be monitored by keeping a check on daily weight. Headaches can also be an indication that the athlete is dehydrated. Thirst, on the other hand, is not a good indicator of dehydration and runners often need to take fluids even when they do not feel thirsty.

Heat Adaptation

The body adapts to heat after about 8-12 days of training in a hot environment by making adjustments to the body's blood flow and sweating processes. During this period the runner will probably feel low on energy as a result of the effect heat has on the utilisation of glycogen stores. During the period of adaptation training should take place, but care needs to be taken to avoid heat related problems.

It will be necessary to reduce the extent and intensity of training loads during the period of adaptation. Care should be taken if training during the hotter times of the day; it may be best to train in the morning or evening when it is cooler. Avoid wearing too much clothing; wear loose clothing which allows air to circulate and light colours which reflect the sun's rays.

Light coloured headgear which gives protection to the head and the neck should be worn. Sufficient fluids should be drunk before, after and during training, and water sprinkled over the head, neck and thighs during runs. Runners should get used to sweating. They should also avoid running immediately after they have eaten as this attracts blood towards the gut and makes the runner less efficient at transferring heat to the body surface.

Warm-ups may be shorter than usual but stretching must not be reduced. Warm-downs are important, to ensure that the runner does not cool down too quickly. Showers and saunas should only be entered after the runner has fully warmed down.

Heat Related Problems

Coaches need to be aware of heat related problems which can occur when runners compete in hot environments when they are not properly prepared. These problems include heat exhaustion, sunstroke and heat stroke.

The symptoms of heat exhaustion are normal skin temperature, cold sweaty skin, drowsiness, weakness, vomiting, an elevated pulse and hypertension. This condition can be avoided by regular drinking of water prior to and during training or competition. A runner who is forced to stop due to heat exhaustion should rest in a cool, airy place and should sip water in order to re-hydrate.

Sunstroke leads to symptoms which include red skin, swollen face, buzzing in the ears, dizziness, headache, nausea, sleepiness, elevated pulse, weakness and rapid respiration. The runner will probably be unable to continue running and may collapse. If, despite sunstroke, the runner manages to continue he may develop heat stroke. A runner with sunstroke should cease all activity and be removed to a cool, well ventilated area; his clothes should be removed and an ice bag or cold compress should be applied to the forehead and the back of the neck.

Heat stroke is the end result of overheating and marks a total breakdown in heat regulation. This rare condition is marked by a high temperature, hot dry red skin, signs of confusion, loss of control, or even collapse. The treatment is to remove the runner to a cool, airy place, undress him and wrap him in a blanket soaked in cold water. Ensure that he has plenty of ventilation. Clear people away from the casualty. It may be necessary to immerse the runner in a bath of cold water to bring the temperature down. If the runner is still conscious, he should be asked to sip water. Medical attention will be necessary in a case of heat stroke.

Adaptation to Altitude

Although British runners only have to compete at altitude occasionally, many endurance athletes go to altitude to train. Due to lower ambient atmospheric pressures, there is less oxygen available to a runner for aerobic activity at altitude. The lower pressure of oxygen in the lungs means that less oxygen can be taken up by the haemoglobin. Training at altitude causes physiological adaptations to take place in response to the shortage of oxygen. These include increased haemoglobin levels and an increased oxygen carrying capacity in the blood. They may also include increased myoglobin levels in the working muscles. These adaptations give the runner a distinct advantage when he returns to sea level, an advantage which is enjoyed by athletes who live at altitude and compete at sea level.

Some athletes choose to live and train at altitude, whilst others travel to altitude two or three times a year for altitude training camps. Training camps need to last a minimum of three weeks and the endurance athlete can expect the adaptations promoted by altitude training to last for about six weeks after his return to sea level. Training needs to take place at heights of 5,000-10,000 feet (1,500-3,000 metres). During the first week of altitude training the training load should be kept low; normal intensity training can be introduced in the second week when acute adaptations to altitude have occurred.

Vo2 Max will fall by about 15-20% at altitude but will slowly rise by about 1% per week at altitude, although it will not rise to pre-altitude levels. There will however be a major improvement in Vo2 Max when the runner returns to sea level.

CHAPTER 8

YOUNG RUNNERS

Endurance competition over a variety of distances is available to young people from an early age and has proved to be a popular activity. Age group competition is officially recognised by British Athletics from eleven years onwards, although schools, youth groups and clubs do provide competitive opportunity earlier. In some cases this is offered from as early as eight years.

Avoid Early Specialisation

The availability of endurance competition from an early age and the ability of the young athlete's physiology to respond to training lures many young runners into early specialisation. Specialisation in endurance running at an early age is not in the best interests of the long term development of an athlete. Athletics, and in particular running, is a healthy activity for young people to participate in. However, early specialisation can put young runners under excessive physical, physiological and psychological pressure and lead to them leaving the sport at a young age. Clearly, a balance needs to be struck between providing young people with the positive experience of participating in endurance activity and providing for their long term development.

Select Appropriate Competition

In the long term, our aim has to be to progress young runners through the age group categories to compete as adults in adult competition. We need to avoid placing so much pressure on young runners that they drop out of the sport before they reach adulthood. For this reason, competition needs to be carefully selected to ensure that it is at an appropriate level for the young runner. Competition is good for young runners provided there is not too much importance placed upon it and its outcome. Unfortunately, many potentially outstanding runners are put off running at an early age by adults including teachers, coaches, club officials, parents and the media, all of whom can place too much importance on competition results.

Adapting to Training Loads

A major problem in coaching young runners is the ease with which they adapt to aerobic training, particularly with pre-pubertal children. Aerobic endurance can be developed at any stage of life, but the relatively low bodyweight of the young runner means that training gains in children are significant. The adaptability of the aerobic system to training has lead in many instances to young runners training like adults. Unfortunately, although the young person's cardio-vascular system adapts well to aerobic endurance training, his musculo-skeletal system, which is still growing, does not cope as well with an excessive volume of training. This leads to many young runners, who are asked to complete inappropriately large training loads, becoming injured.

Pubertal Endurance Changes

Training pre-pubertal runners aerobically is also highly specific, as young people at this stage of development appear not to be capable of performing much work anaerobically. Many young runners experience improvement when they train aerobically prior to puberty. This rate of improvement declines rapidly after puberty, if training is not adjusted to take account of the runner's new found ability to work anaerobically. After puberty, training needs to shift from being almost totally aerobic to a mixture of aerobic and anaerobic work. Implied here is not just anaerobic endurance but also factors such as speed, strength and mobility.

Girls, in particular, experience major problems after puberty. In most cases, there is an increase in their relative bodyweight in the form of an increase in percentage body fat. This makes them less efficient aerobically at a stage when the middle distance events they compete in are becoming less aerobic and more anaerobic. Unless these changes are shadowed by a change in the approach to training, girls are likely to experience a drop off in performance ability. The changes in maximal oxygen uptake in girls and boys as a result of growth are shown in Figure 91.

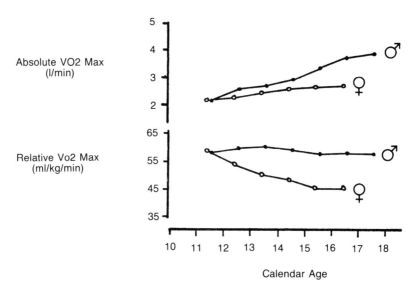

Fig. 91 Changes in maximal aerobic power with maturation. (Adapted from Kemper and Verschuur.)

Stages of Development

A knowledge of the stages of development young runners pass through, as they progress from being children to adults, is essential for all who work with age group participants. Giving precise ages to the various stages of development for young people is impossible due to the variation between individuals in terms of maturation rate. One girl, for example, might reach puberty at 12 years of age whilst another might be 18 years. The following estimates of the age at which various changes occur are open to wide individual variation.

Puberty is reached in girls on average two to three years earlier than boys.

In girls this may be between eleven and thirteen years, and in boys between fourteen and sixteen years. Prior to puberty, both males and females have similar relative Vo2 Max values. After puberty, the relative value of Vo2 Max for girls declines and for boys it continues to develop.

Around puberty, there is a rapid rise in female oestrogen hormones in girls, while in boys there is an increase in male androgen hormones. Oestrogen discourages muscle adaptation to training, whilst androgen encourages muscle adaptation. The post pubertal female athlete will find adaptation to strength training more difficult than her male counterpart, who will respond well to this type of exercise.

Skeletal growth ends in females at about eighteen years and in males at about twenty-one years. Prior to this the bones, in particular the growing ends of the long bones and the bones of the spine, are easily damaged.

The Growing Runner

Although differing maturation rates make prescription of the development of the young runner difficult, the following table is offered as a guide. The approach offered in this table assumes that the young runner will pass through three distinct phases. The first is a foundation period which can start as early as nine and can last until about fourteen. The second is a developmental period, running from thirteen/fourteen to seventeen/twenty-two years, and the third following on from there is the period of adult participation.

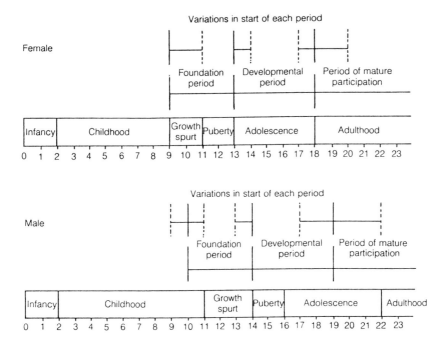

Fig. 92 Stages of development and training phases.

89

Foundation Period

— 9/11 — 13/14 years.

— 3-4 years duration.

— emphasis on games, fun activities, variety of activity.

— general training, skill development and speed development are priorities.

— aerobic endurance, strength development using bodyweight and mobility are key conditioning areas.

— develop basic skills and rhythm.

— one training session per week, increasing to three per week.

— competition should be limited, varied, should include award schemes and should be free from major pressures. Competitions such as championship and representative fixtures are not appropriate for this age range.

Developmental Period

— 13/14 — 17/22 years.

— 4-6 years duration.

— emphasis on general training in first years.

— percentage of specific training gradually increases over last two years.

— develop appropriate training and competition behaviours.

— teach weight training techniques with 60% maximum loadings.

— three training sessions per week, gradually increasing to six per week in later years.

— increasing importance placed on formal competition. Championships and representative fixtures introduced as the runner advances through this stage.

Period of Mature Participation

— 17-22 years plus.

— not before 17 or after 22.

— percentage of specific work increases.

— time spent in training increases significantly, especially for the elite athlete.

— frequency and difficulty of competition increases.

Training Guidelines

Aerobic Endurance

Aerobic training can be introduced from an early age. Care should be taken to limit the duration of training runs and the frequency of training sessions for very young runners. As a guide, the following table offers suggestions on the maximum volume of aerobic training for different ages.

Aerobic training for young athletes will involve continuous, varied pace and intermittent methods. The volume of training should be kept relatively low and quality of training is emphasised.

Age	Club Runner	Elite Runner
9		
10	Limited to a maximum	
11	of 2 × 20 min runs/week	
12		
13	10-15 miles/week	
14	10-15 miles/week	15-20 miles/week
15	10-20 miles/week	15-20 miles/week
16	20 miles/week	25-30 miles/week
17	25 miles/week	30-40 miles/week
18	30 miles/week	40-50 miles/week

Table 12: *Recommended volume of endurance training for young runners aged 9-18 years.*

Anaerobic Endurance

Anaerobic training should be introduced after puberty and, as with aerobic training, the volumes will be relatively low and the quality high. Sufficient recovery should be allowed in specific endurance training to enable the young athlete to maintain quality.

Variety in Endurance Training

Variety is a key factor when working with young athletes. Using a variety in training sessions helps keep young runners motivated and also reduces the likelihood of over-use injuries. Training should take place in differing environments using a variety of running surfaces.

The following running sessions are designed to bring variety to continuous, varied pace and intermittent training methods.

1. *Whistle fartlek*
   Coach uses whistle to indicate pre-planned pace.

2. *Indian file fartlek*
   The squad run spaced 5-10m apart, and the last man sprints to front of file. Variations include weaving in and out of the squad of runners or two runners together on either side of file.

3. *Terrain fartlek*
   Coach puts squad out over a pre-set course with set cues such as run hard uphill, sprint on flat sections, jog downhill, etc.

4. *Fox and hounds fartlek*
   A fox or various foxes are given a lead in a restricted area and the other athletes must catch them.

5. *Continuous relays*
   Using a 400m track or circuit and team of 5 runners. Runners 1 and 5 stand at the start/finish, 2 at 100m, 3 at 200m, 4 at 300m. Run for a set time or for a set number of laps.

6. *Paarlauf*

A continuous relay with 2 runners. On a 400m track the first runner runs 200m and passes baton to second runner who also runs 200m. Whilst this runner is completing the 200m stretch, the partner jogs across the track back to his starting point to receive the baton.

7. *Timed team runs*

Decide on a set time, say 30 seconds; place flags from 150m to 200m at 10m intervals. Blow a whistle for start and finish of 30 second period. Athletes run for 30 seconds and are awarded points for their team according to which flag they reach.

Skill

Training to develop the skill of sprinting should feature in all young athletes' training programmes, along with the development of other skills including hurdling. The practices outlined in Chapter 4 are appropriate for use with young runners.

Age	Distance	Number of Hurdles	Number of Water Jumps
15-17	1500 metres	13	3
17-20	2000 metres	18	5
20 +	3000 metres	28	7

Table 13: *Number of hurdles and water jumps for various steeplechase events.*

* Note: The first hurdle in a 1500m will be hurdle 4 and the first hurdle in a 2000m will be hurdle 3.

Mobility

As mobility starts to decline in young people from about eight years of age, mobility training should be included in the young runner's programme. A variety of exercises involving all of the body's joint actions should be practised on a regular basis. The programme of mobility exercises shown in Chapter 3 will develop all-round mobility rather than specific mobility for running, and this programme would be appropriate for young athletes. Young athletes should be taught how to perform active mobility exercises. Passive and kinetic exercises should only be undertaken when there is trained supervision available.

Strength

During the foundation period, strength training can take the form of partner games, climbing activities, hopping relays, games with benches, boxes, medicine balls, etc. Torso exercises which strengthen the musculature of the spine, such as abdominals, back extension, lateral bends and rotations should be included. One unit of strength training per week will suffice and it should include a large variety of exercises.

A more formal approach to strength training is taken in the developmental period. Circuit training, with its progression of repetitions and sets, is used. Exercises need to be carefully selected to ensure that all of the major muscle groups are strengthened. Simple exercises are chosen and they need to be well taught, ensuring a good range of movement. The sets, repetitions and recovery periods should be calculated to allow the runner to maintain the quality of movement in each exercise.

Weight training is introduced around sixteen to seventeen years of age, possibly using the multi-gym as a starting point, and keeping repetitions high at first. The techniques of lifting free weights should be taught using loads of about 60% of maximum. Athletic exercises such as power cleans, snatch, half squats, and bench press should be used with repetitions of greater than eight. Plyometric exercises, hopping and bounding activities are also introduced at this stage.

Strength training for young runners should emphasise exercises which work those muscles which stabilise the hip/spine, and add stability to rotation of the spine. Loadings on the spine and the knees need to be kept low; weights should not be supported on the back, and depth jumps should not be performed until the runner reaches the age of sixteen. As young runners are motivated by weight training, a coach/teacher needs to supervise this aspect of training to keep over-enthusiasm in check and to encourage gradual progress.

CHAPTER 9
FEMALE RUNNERS

It was really only in the sixties that women started to be allowed to compete in the endurance running events with the re-introduction of the 800m to the Olympic programme. Prior to this, the longest recognised running event for women was the 400m. The seventies saw the addition at international level of the 1500m and 3000m, and in the eighties the 10,000m and marathon. Today previously held fears about the dangers of women taking part in endurance competition have been discredited and women train for and compete in endurance events on equal terms with the men.

Training

In broad terms, women train for endurance running in a similar manner to men. The female runner wishing to reach the top in any of the endurance events must be prepared to devote the same amount of time to training as do top male runners. She will use the same training methods, and her training loads will be completed at the same relative intensity and will involve a similar volume to those of men with equivalent best performances. Any differences in the training load will relate to performance levels rather than to gender.

Differences which occur are related to the lower levels of aerobic endurance and strength found in women. These differences affect more the balance rather than the composition of training, as is reflected in the annual training plan. Here more attention is given to training to develop aerobic endurance and strength at key stages of the plan.

Physiological Differences

It would be wrong to dwell too long on the physiological differences between male and female runners for there are more similarities than differences. Nevertheless, differences in aerobic power and strength do exist, requiring these areas to be given special attention in training. The differences in aerobic power are well illustrated by the following Vo2 Max values.

Elite female runners   —   65-75 ml/kg/min.
Elite male runners   —   75-85 ml/kg/min.

The differences in aerobic power between men and women are related to the women's lower oxygen carrying and utilisation capacity and to the influence of higher percentages of body fat on relative aerobic efficiency. Female runners therefore require to place a greater emphasis on the development of aerobic endurance, allocating more time to this in the annual training plan. Improvements in aerobic fitness take longer to develop, perhaps explaining why many women continue to be successful in endurance events well into their 30's. They also lose aerobic endurance at a faster rate than men, and therefore need to include sufficient amounts of this type of training to maintain fitness during competition periods.

Unlike aerobic endurance, there are no differences in anaerobic endurance capacity, the ability to produce lactic acid being similar in both men and women. Anaerobic training therefore is the same as that used by male runners.

Strength differences between men and women are related to the presence of the female hormone, oestrogen, which discourages muscle hypertrophy. This is compared with the male runner's high percentage of the male hormone, androgen, which encourages hypertrophy and strength development. Women therefore need to include more strength training in their annual plans than do the majority of male runners.

Reproductive Function

The menstrual cycle can influence running performance, and equally running can influence the menstrual cycle. The runner with a regular cycle may find that physical and emotional changes detract from her running performance. Other runners may experience changes to or loss of their menstrual cycle as a result of training.

Those runners with a regular cycle may experience physical and emotional changes in the days immediately prior to menstruation. These changes may include abdominal pain, retention of fluid leading to increased body weight, increased risk of injury, increased irritability and decreased coordination and concentration. Such changes in turn lead to a temporary deterioration in running performance. A record of the runner's menstrual cycle should be kept in order that comparison can be made between the cycle and training and competition performance. A diary such as the one shown in Table 14 can be used to monitor the cycle, weight changes and how the runner feels. If performance levels are affected negatively during the pre-menstrual phase or menstruation itself and the cycle is likely to fall on important competitive dates, assistance can be sought from a gynaecologist to alter or re-schedule the cycle. On a more positive note, some runners find that training reduces pre-menstrual symptoms and increases their pain threshold.

Participation in endurance training can affect the menstrual function of runners. In young females, commencement of menstruation (the menarche) may be delayed as a consequence of endurance training. Tall slim girls possess the ideal frame for endurance running. Such girls tend to reach the menarche late, but this may be further delayed as a result of training or nutritional factors. Some girls may only reach menarche after an enforced lay-off due to injury. If the menarche is not reached by 16 years of age, it is advisable to consult with a gynaecologist.

Delays in reaching menarche, irregular menstrual periods and the loss of menstruation (secondary amenorrhoea) may be due to low body fat levels, nutritional factors and stress. One of the hormones which controls the menstrual cycle is partly produced in the body fat. A low percentage body fat causes a low level in the body of this hormone, which in turn leads to menstrual dysfunction. It is estimated that 50% of competitive female runners experience amenorrhoea.

Osteoporosis

The loss of regular menstrual function may have short term benefits such as an absence of pre-menstrual symptoms, increased relative aerobic power and increased relative strength. In the long term, though, there are major concerns regarding the strength of bones of amenorrhoeic women.

Exercise is generally thought to strengthen bones and to reduce fracture risk. In women, the risk of fracturing bones increases greatly after about 50 years

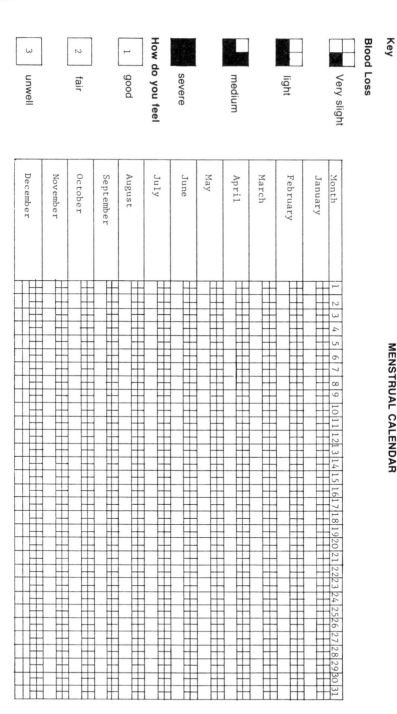

MENSTRUAL CALENDAR

Key

Blood Loss

Very slight	
light	
medium	
severe	

How do you feel

1 good

2 fair

3 unwell

Month	1	2	3	4	5	6	7	8	9	10	11	12	13	14	15	16	17	18	19	20	21	22	23	24	25	26	27	28	29	30	31
January																															
February																															
March																															
April																															
May																															
June																															
July																															
August																															
September																															
October																															
November																															
December																															

Table 14: *Menstrual cycle record.*

of age. This is due to a condition known as osteoporosis or brittle bone disease. The same condition is found in amenorrhoeic women, making them susceptible to stress fractures and other bone/muscle injuries.

The bone density of amenorrhoeic women at age 25 has been found to be as low as that of women twice their age. Women reach their peak bone strength somewhere between 20 and 30 years of age. Although it is not known what the long term effects of osteoporosis might be, amenorrhoeic athletes are advised to check with their doctor as some form of hormone replacement may be advisable. In addition, all female athletes should monitor their calcium intake which is often low. The recommended daily intake of calcium is 1000mg per day, but should be 1500mg per day for female runners with irregular menstrual cycles. Dairy products are very high in calcium — milk has 125gm per 2100ml and yoghurt has 144mg per 100g.

Female runners may also need to supplement iron and vitamin C as they are prone to anaemia at certain stages of their menstrual cycle. A doctor with an interest in running should be asked to monitor haemoglobin levels and to prescribe iron if necessary. It may also be advisable for female runners to supplement the B vitamins which are involved in energy metabolism, especially if the runner is using oral contraceptives.

Eating Disorders

The advantages to performance of reduced body weight and a lowered percentage body fat may lead to female athletes reducing their calorie intake. Such nutritional strategies often develop into abnormal eating habits in highly motivated female runners. There would appear to be a high incidence amongst female runners of eating disorders such as anorexia nervosa and bulemia. These conditions, which may also be due to other pressures such as a poor body image, will require medical assistance and strong support to be overcome. Coaches should be careful not to over-stress weight loss with female runners and, if dietary control is needed, to recruit a nutritionist to advise on this. If coaches suspect that one of the female runners they are working with does have an eating disorder, they should recruit medical advice.

Fig. 93 Running action — Yvonne Murray (G.B.), Maricica Puica (Romania) and Zola Budd (G.B.).

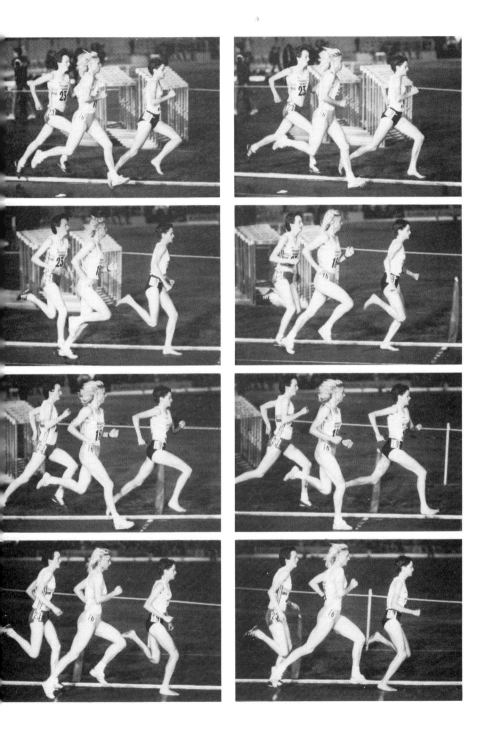

CHAPTER 10
NUTRITION

Nutrition is an important factor in endurance running. It provides the energy needed for competition and training, promotes recovery and enables the body's metabolic processes to function properly. The importance of an appropriate diet to endurance performance ranks alongside hereditary factors and training.

Energy

The energy which comes from food may be measured in kilocalories or, using a more modern system, kilojoules. The kilocalorie is commonly referred to as a calorie. The daily amount of calories required by each individual will vary in the normal adult population from around 2000 to 3500 calories. The individual's requirements depend on the metabolic rate, size, energy demands of work and energy demands of training. If a runner is maintaining his/her weight, it is an indication that the calories being consumed are balanced with those being expended. If however a runner requires to lose weight, to gain weight, or is losing or gaining weight unintentionally, the diet will require to be altered accordingly in order to adjust the calorie balance.

Carbohydrate

During exercise such as running, the body prefers to use carbohydrate as its main source of energy. A carbohydrate rich diet is therefore essential, both during training and prior to competition, to ensure that carbohydrate stores in the body are maintained. Failure to do this will lead to reduced performances in training and competition. A runner training on depleted stores of carbohydrate will not gain maximum benefit from training.

In the food we consume there are two types of carbohydrate, starch and sugar. Sugar (confectionery, lemonade, sugar) and starch (bread, pasta, fruit, vegetables) will produce the same amount of energy. However, starch is considered to be a better form of carbohydrate, as it is accompanied by vitamins and minerals. These are missing from sugary foods, hence the reference to sweet foodstuffs, which lack vitamins and minerals, as empty calories. Starches and sugars are broken down and stored in the body as liver glycogen, blood glucose or muscle glycogen.

Muscle glycogen is broken down to ATP for use as energy by both aerobic and anaerobic processes. When working aerobically, the oxygen cost, the amount of oxygen that will be used to convert a gram of carbohydrate, is 0.7 litres. This produces four calories of energy and means that each calorie has taken 0.175 litres of oxygen to produce. This compares with a cost per calorie of 0.225 litres of oxygen to convert fats to ATP. As it takes less oxygen to convert carbohydrate to energy than fats, the body will if it has the choice use carbohydrate as the main source of energy during aerobic activity. There is however a limited supply of carbohydrate stored in the body. At a steady running speed it is estimated that the body's carbohydrate stores would only sustain about 100 mins of activity if they were used as the major fuel source.

Fats

In long distance running events such as the marathon, fats become an important source of energy in order that carbohydrate can be spared for other essential functions. Stores of fats in the body are large enough to provide the body's energy demands for several days. At rest, they provide up to 70% of the body's energy needs, and with low intensity running will provide about 50% of the energy required. Training of a low intensity and a long duration will train the body to utilise a greater amount of fats as energy, helping to spare carbohydrate. Marathon runners can, through long slow distance work, shift the proportion of energy supplied by fats during a long distance run from 50% to 60-70%.

As a nutrient, fats have several other important roles in addition to being a source of energy. They provide insulation, protect the vital organs, supply certain vitamins, and make food both appetising and filling. Consumption of fats is important to the health of the body; however, too much fat in the diet can also be a health hazard. Fats are associated with cardio-vascular disease. For better health, vegetable or polyunsaturated fats are preferred in the diet to animal or saturated fats.

Protein

Protein can also be a source of energy, but it is generally ignored as such when there is a plentiful supply of carbohydrate and fats. A nitrogen rich compound, protein is formed by amino acids and is involved mainly in growth and the repair of damaged tissues. It has a role in the metabolic process that converts both carbohydrate and fats into energy, and in helping the body to tolerate the build-up of lactic acid produced during anaerobic activity. Protein is a key structural component of the cells, antibodies, enzymes and hormones. It is involved in the production of haemoglobin and the enzymes involved in energy liberation. It also plays a role in maintaining the body's osmotic balance.

Protein in food comes in the form of amino acids, of which there are twenty-two. Eight of these cannot be manufactured in the body and have to be found in the food. Foods which contain all of the essential amino acids in the proper ratio and in sufficient quantities are called complete protein foods. These are milk, meat, fish, poultry and eggs. Incomplete protein foods such as vegetables, fruit and grains are missing one or more of the essential amino acids. It is possible, by careful mixing of incomplete protein foods, to ensure that the body gets sufficient amounts of all of the essential amino acids. This however requires special dietary care which may be beyond the capabilities of many runners. Care therefore needs to be taken with runners who are vegetarian to ensure that their diet is providing all of the essential amino acids.

Vitamins

Vitamins are unrelated organic compounds contained in the food we eat, which play important roles in allowing our bodies to function properly. The various chemical processes which regulate the body, release energy and repair tissues all involve vitamins.

The water soluble vitamins, B and C, play an important role in energy and protein metabolism. It is thought they are depleted as a result of strenuous training. Runners therefore need to ensure that their diets include food sources

Vitamin	Function	Good Sources	RDA
A	Growth, repair, eyes, skin, fights infection, aids energy production.	Margarine, butter, milk, liver, carrots, egg yolk, green leafy veg., yellow veg., fruits.	800-1000ug
D	Calcium — bone formation.	Sunshine, margarine, butter, egg yolk, fish oil.	10ug
E	Protects vitamins and essential free fatty acids.	Wheatgerm, egg, vegetable oil.	8-10mg
K	Blood clotting.	Green vegetables, liver, meats, soya beans.	70-140ug

Table 15: *Fat soluble vitamins.*

containing these vitamins. These vitamins may also be destroyed in food processing and cooking. This would suggest that fresh vegetables and fruit be included in the diet and that care is taken to avoid over-cooking vegetables.

If there is an adequate supply of vitamins in the athlete's diet there should not be a need to take vitamin supplements. Some runners may feel the need to take supplements. Vitamins B and C, being water soluble, can be supplemented safely as excess intake is merely passed out in the urine. Care needs to be taken in supplementing fat soluble vitamins as excess dosages cannot be expelled from the body and may lead to vitamin toxicity.

Minerals

Like vitamins, minerals play an important role in the body's metabolic processes. There are 17 essential minerals; those whose RDA exceeds 100 milligrams/day are known as macro-minerals and those with a lesser RDA are known as micro-minerals or trace elements. The macro-minerals are calcium, phosphorous, magnesium, potassium, sulphur, sodium and chlorine. The micro-minerals include iron, zinc, selenium, manganese, copper, iodine, molybdenum, cobalt, fluorine, and chromium.

Most minerals are well provided for in the diet, three possible exceptions being calcium, iron and zinc. Calcium accounts for about 40% of the body's clotting, transportation of fluids and muscle enzyme activity. The RDA for calcium is 500mg but women are recommended to take 1000mg, and amenorrhoeic women 1500mg. Sources of calcium include milk, dairy products, green vegetables, bread and nuts.

Iron (RDA of 12mg) plays a critical role in the oxygen transport system. Oxygen is carried in the blood stream by haemoglobin which is a protein containing iron. In the muscle, haemoglobin releases its oxygen to a substance called myoglobin which also contains iron. A shortage of iron, anaemia, in the body has a profound effect on the runner's oxygen carrying capacity. It is common for runners to be anaemic, especially women. Regular blood tests to monitor the body's total iron content should be conducted. If a runner is

Vitamin	Function	Good Sources	RDA
B1 (Thiamine)	Energy metabolism and nervous system.	Brown bread, milk, vegetables, potatoes, meat, pulses, eggs, cheese, fish, fowl.	1-1.5mg
B2 (Riboflavine)	Energy and protein metabolism.	Milk and milk products, brown bread, meat, fish, green veg., eggs.	1.2-1.7ug
B3 (Niacin)	Energy metabolism, free fatty acid production.	Brown bread, meat, fish, fowl, peanuts.	13-19mg
B5 (Pantothenic acid)	Haemoglobin formation and carbohydrate, fats and protein metabolism.	Wholegrain cereals, organ meats, eggs.	4-7mg
B6 (Pyridoxine)	Protein metabolism.	Bread, milk, eggs, veg., nuts, meat, fish, fowl.	1.8-2.2mg
B12 (Cobalamin)	Red blood cell production, nervous system, energy and metabolism.	Meat, liver, milk, eggs.	3-4ug
Biotin	Carbohydrate, fat and protein metabolism.	Liver, peanuts, yeast, milk, egg yolk, cereal, bananas, grapefruit, tomatoes.	100-200ug
Folic Acid	Blood cell production, growth, protein metabolism.	Liver, raw green veg., pulses.	400ug
C (Ascorbic acid)	Fights infection, iron, protein and energy metabolism.	Fresh fruit, veg.	30-1000mg

Table 16: *Water soluble vitamins.*

found to be anaemic, then iron supplements may need to be prescribed under medical supervision. Care needs to be taken in supplementing iron as excess iron levels can lead to a toxic condition. If iron is prescribed, it should be taken with vitamin C which promotes iron absorption. Symptoms of anaemia in runners include a lack of colour, deterioration in training and racing performance, headaches, difficulty with sleep and breathlessness. Food sources of iron include brown bread, meat, vegetables and pulses.

Zinc (RDA of 15mg) is a constituent of essential enzymes and, along with copper, is involved in the production of haemoglobin. It should only be supplemented under medical supervision. Food sources rich in zinc include milk, lean muscle meat, green vegetables, liver, fish and wheatbran.

Water

Second only to oxygen in maintaining life, water makes up 60% of the human body. It requires to be constantly replaced to maintain fluid balance. Fluid loss or dehydration leading to losses of 15-20% can be fatal. Water is necessary for most bodily functions including the digestion, absorption, circulation and excretion processes. In exercise, it maintains an electrolyte balance and it is involved in transporting the nutrients.

Thirst is not a good indicator of fluid requirements, especially in hot conditions where it fails to keep up with the body's needs. In circumstances where we have increased exercise or hot climates, there is a need for constant replacement of water. Here it is better to drink too much rather than too little. In moderate conditions the body needs to replace about 2 litres per day.

Fibre

Although it has no direct influence on endurance performance, fibre is essential for better health. Fibre may however cause athletes to feel bulky.

Alcohol

Alcohol is a source of energy; however it cannot be used by the muscles during exercise and is therefore converted to fat. It also causes dehydration and mineral loss, which can have a negative effect on performance. Although it is in moderation a relaxant, alcohol is generally not recommended for serious runners, especially not prior to competition.

The Runner's Diet

It is generally accepted that the diet recommended for healthy life is appropriate for athletes. Such a diet is high in carbohydrate, and is rich in foods which contain vitamins and minerals.

Protein	11%
Fats	25%-30%
Carbohydrate	55-60% (Sugar 10%)
	(Starch 45-50%)
Fibre	30 grams/day
Salt	5 grams/day

There may be times when exhaustive training or competition demands intakes of carbohydrate as high as 70%.

One of the problems facing runners is how to equate their daily diet with the recommended RDA's. This can best be achieved by the athlete consulting a dietician. A dietary diary can be kept over a number of days to record the amount of food being consumed by the athlete. This can then be analysed by computer to identify the runner's actual intake in terms of calories and nutrients. A comparison with the actual amounts of nutrients consumed and the RDA's will identify any dietary deficiencies. The dietician can then use this information to give the runner practical advice as to how to change his diet to make up for these deficiencies.

If it is not possible to undergo a full dietary analysis, the following table may be of use to runners.

Food Groups	Daily Amounts for Adults
Milk & milk products	Two or more servings per day, either as a milk drink or a milk product, such as cheese and ice cream. A serving would be one cup or its equivalent.
Meat and high protein products	Two or more servings of meat, fish, poultry, eggs or vegetables, such as dried beans, lentils, peas and nuts. A serving of meat, fish or poultry would be 3.5 ounces of lean and boneless meat.
Fruit and vegetables	Four or more servings per day of $\frac{1}{2}$ cup or more.
Cereal and grain	Four or more servings per day, with one serving equal to one slice of bread, $\frac{1}{2}$ to $\frac{3}{4}$ cup of cooked cereal, macaroni, spaghetti, etc.

The Pre-Competition Diet

The main requirement prior to competition is that the athlete's glycogen stores are high and that he/she is well hydrated. The pre-competition meal should not be too large and should be of a high carbohydrate content. As adrenalin will flow as the athlete approaches competition, causing the digestive system to shut down, it is best that the pre-competition meal is taken 3-4 hours prior to competition. Fluids, especially water, can be taken right up to the start of the race.

Competitions often take place away from home, forcing athletes to eat out. Care should be taken in the choice of restaurants and new foods should be avoided, just in case these disagree with the runner.

Competition Diet

In races over 10,000m, refreshments, water and sponge stations can be provided. Water stations are provided every five kilometres in marathon races and it is recommended that athletes drink about 150-200ml of water at each one. Dehydration is a major problem in all long distance events, even more so if the conditions are hot and humid. As dehydration leads to heat stress and reduced performance, it is important to replace fluid lost through sweating.

In marathon championships the runners can supply their own drinks for each of the refreshment stations. The recommended marathon drink will provide both water and carbohydrate. Provided a mild solution of a complex carbohydrate is used, the presence of the carbohydrate should not interfere with the uptake of the fluid from the gut. The recommended solutions will contain about 3% carbohydrate.

A similar drink might also be useful for track athletes who are unable to eat between rounds of a competition.

105

Post-Training / Competition Diet

After training and competition, the nutritional priority is to replace fluid and carbohydrate as soon as possible. Within ten minutes of completing the training session or competition, the athlete should drink a carbohydrate drink. The first meal after training/competition should be taken within an hour-and-a-half to two hours. The meal should be rich in carbohydrate, protein, vitamins and minerals. Fruit juice is useful in replacing fluid and minerals lost.

Marathon Diet

In the past many marathon runners have followed a particular training and dietary regimen during the week prior to a race in order to glycogen load. This involved the runner completing an exhaustive run to deplete his carbohydrate stores about seven days before the race. This was followed by three days of a diet where the runner consumed mainly fat and protein and deprived the body of carbohydrate. In the remaining three days before the race the runner changed to a carbohydrate rich diet. The effect of this procedure was to increase the muscle stores of muscle glycogen to twice normal levels.

There is little doubt that this approach leads to increased glycogen levels in the muscles. It is however stressful, and it can result in the runner becoming irritable, falling prey to colds, etc and suffering from problems such as diarrhoea, dehydration and fatigue. Such symptoms prior to running a marathon would not be conducive to better performance.

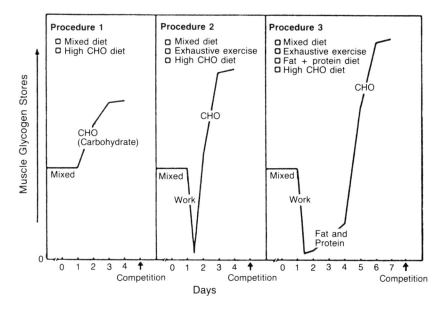

Fig. 94 Effects of nutritional/training strategies on muscle glycogen stores. (Adapted from Saltin and Hermansen.)

Recent research has shown that there is no need to undertake the depletion run or to starve the body of carbohydrate for 3-4 days prior to increasing the

106

intake of carbohydrate. Increasing carbohydrate intake during the last 3-4 days prior to the marathon will in itself produce increased levels of muscle glycogen similar to those produced by the traditional approach, but without the side effects.

Our advice to the marathon runner is to taper down training over a 7-10 day period prior to the race and, during the last 3-4 days, to keep training at a minimum but to increase the carbohydrate and fluid intake.

CHAPTER 11
HISTORY

British Running — 20th Century Success

Great Britain and Northern Ireland runners have established an enviable tradition in middle distance running and steeplechasing with remarkable success throughout this century. These are some of the important landmarks.

1900-1909

Alfred Tysoe wins the 800m at the 1900 Olympic Games in Paris after some Americans refuse to contest the final as it is being held on a Sunday. Charles Bennett wins the 1500m and also finishes first in the 5000m, a team event won by Britain. There are two steeplechase races held and the longer race over a 4000m course produces a clean sweep for British runners with John Rimmer winning, Charles Bennett taking second and Sidney Robinson third. In the other race, held over a 2500m course, Sidney Robinson goes one better, winning the silver medal.

Alfred Shrubb sets inaugural world records for 3 miles (in 1903), for 6 miles and for 10,000m (in 1904).

Britain's Olympic success continues in the steeplechase with John Daly taking the silver medal over a 2590m course in 1904 and Arthur Russell and Archie Robertson taking first and second places over a 3200m course in 1908.

Wyndham Halswelle (the controversial winner of the 400m in 1908 when his American opponents refuse to take part in a re-run) finishes third in the 800m at the 1906 Olympic Games. John McGough wins a silver medal in the 1500m in 1906 and Henry Hawtrey triumphs in the 5 miles. In 1908, Harold Wilson and Norman Hallows finish second and third respectively in that event, while Emil Voigt and Edward Owen win gold and silver medals in a 5 mile race. The British quintet take first place in the 3 mile team race with Joe Deakin the individual winner.

1910-1919

At the 1912 Olympic Games in Stockholm, Arnold Jackson wins the 1500m. Bronze medals are won by George Hutson in the 5000m and by the British teams in the 3000m team race and the cross-country team race.

In 1912, as in 1906, there is no steeplechase included in the Olympic Games.

1920-29

Albert Hill beats favourite and 400m winner Bevil Rudd of South Africa in the 1920 Antwerp Olympic Games 800m. The 31-year-old then goes on to achieve a double by winning the 1500m, a feat not to be repeated again until 1964, by Peter Snell. Philip Baker finishes second to Hill in the 1500m, James Wilson wins bronze at 10,000m and British teams gain silver medals in two team events, at 3000m and cross-country. At the same Olympics, Percy Hodge wins the 3000m steeplechase.

Douglas Lowe wins the 800m at the 1924 Olympic Games in Paris and then retains his title at the 1928 Games in Amsterdam. Henry Stallard wins a bronze medal in the 1500m at the Paris Games, while silver medals for the 3000m team event are also won by Britain.

It is at the 1928 Olympic Games that the 800m is introduced for the first time as a women's event. Few of the competitors have prepared to run the distance and most finish the final in a distressed state. There is an outcry about the suitability of women running an event which is as long as 800m, and as a result the event is dropped from the Olympic programme.

1930-1939

At the 1932 Olympic Games, a bespectacled runner, Thomas Hampson, edges out Canadian athlete Alex Wilson to win the 800m in a world record time of 1:49.8. John Cornes takes the silver in the 1500m, and Tom Evenson finishes second in the steeplechase which is run over 3460m as judges miscount the laps.

At the 1932 Games in Los Angeles Sam Ferris takes the silver medal in the marathon, a feat repeated by Ernie Harper at the Berlin Games in 1936.

In 1937 Sydney Wooderson sets a World Record for the mile of 4:06.4. The following year he lowers the 800m record to 1:48.4 and wins the European 1500m Championship in Paris.

1940-1949

The Second World War hits middle and long distance running in Britain. Our only gold medal at the 1946 European Championships in Oslo is won by Sydney Wooderson in the 5000m, and the only medal forthcoming at the 1948 Olympic Games in London is again a silver in the marathon, this time for Tom Richards.

1950-1959

Britain wins four medals in endurance events at the 1950 European Championships in Brussels. Jack Holden wins the marathon, John Parlett wins the 800m ahead of Roger Bannister who takes bronze, and Bill Nankeville finishes third in the 1500m.

Roger Bannister just fails to win a medal in finishing fourth in the 1500m in the 1952 Olympic Games in Helsinki. John Disley wins the bronze medal in the 3000m steeplechase. In 1953 Gordon Pirie sets a new world 6 miles record.

Roger Bannister becomes the first man to run the Mile in under 4 minutes on Thursday, 6th May 1954, when he runs 3:59.4 at the AAA versus Oxford University Match at Iffley Road, Oxford. Freddie Green and Chris Chataway break the world 3 mile record at the AAA Championships. Chataway then makes the 3 mile and 5000m records his own.

Roger Bannister wins the 1500m at the 1954 European Championships in Berne. Other UK medal winners are Chris Chataway second in the 5000m, Frank Sando third in the 10,000m and Diane Leather second in the inaugural women's 800m. Diane becomes the first woman in the world to run a sub 5 minute mile, and improves the record again in the following year.

At the 1956 Olympic Games in Melbourne, Chris Brasher wins the 3000m steeplechase and Derek Johnson is runner-up in the 800m. Gordon Pirie and Derek Ibbotson take silver and bronze in the 5000m. Pirie sets 3 world records in the one year, at 3000m (twice) and 5000m.

Derek Ibbotson breaks the world mile record in 1957, running 3:57.2.

Brian Hewson wins the 1500m at the 1958 European Championships in Stockholm and Mike Rawson the 800m after an appeal against disqualification. Gordon Pirie takes third in the 5000m and Fred Norris third in the marathon. Diane Leather repeats her placing from the previous championships by again finishing second in the 800m.

1960-1969

At the 1960 Olympic Games in Rome the women's 800m is reintroduced, having been dropped 32 years before.

Bruce Tulloh wins the 5000m at the 1962 European Championships in Belgrade and Roy Fowler finishes third in the 10,000m. The marathon is won by Brian Kilby.

In Tokyo at the 1964 Olympic Games, Ann Packer who is considered an outsider wins the 800m comfortably in 2:01.1 ahead of the favourite, Dupureur of France.

Maurice Herriott wins a silver medal at the Tokyo Games in the steeplechase, as does Basil Heatley in the marathon.

Jim Hogan wins the marathon at the 1966 European Championships in Budapest, only his third race over the distance. In 1967 Ann Smith improves the world records for 1 mile and 1500m.

There are golds for John Whetton (1500m), Ian Stewart (5000m), Ron Hill (marathon) and Lillian Board (800m) at the 1969 European Championships in Athens. Mike Tagg is second in the 10,000m, Alan Blinston is third in the 5000m and Jim Alder is third in the marathon.

1970-1979

At the 1971 European Championships in Helsinki Trevor Wright takes the silver medal in the marathon ahead of Ron Hill who collects the bronze medal. In the women's 800m, Pat Lowe and Rosemary Stirling also finish second and third. Andy Carter is third in the men's 800m and Brendan Foster is third in the 1500m.

At the 1972 Olympic Games in Munich Ian Stewart wins the bronze medal in the 5000m, an achievement equalled by Brendan Foster in the 10,000m at the 1976 Games in Montreal.

In 1973 David Bedford improves the world record for 10,000m to 27:30.8. Brendan Foster lowers the world record for 2 miles, and in the following year achieves new figures for 3000m.

Brendan Foster wins the 5000m at the 1974 European Championships in Rome and Ian Thompson wins the marathon. There are silver medals for Steve Ovett in the 800m, Tony Simmons in the 10,000m and a bronze medal for Joyce Smith in the first women's 3000m.

Steve Ovett wins the 1500m at the 1978 European Championships in Prague and takes the silver medal in the 800m. Sebastian Coe is third in the 800m and David Moorcroft is third in the 1500m.

Sebastian Coe sets the mould for the 1980's when he sets world records in 1979 at 800m (1:42.4), 1500m (3:32.1) and mile (3:49.0).

1980-1989

Against most predictions Steve Ovett wins the 1980 Moscow Olympic Games' 800m and Sebastian Coe the 1500m. Ovett takes the bronze in the 1500m and Coe the silver in the 800m.

During 1980, Steve Ovett equals Sebastian Coe's world record for the 1500m, a time that he improves later that year to 3:31.36. Ovett also betters Coe's mile record, lowering it to 3:48.8. Coe sets a new record for 1000m, improving it again in the following year.

In 1981, Sebastian Coe improves his 1981 800m world record to 1:41.73. In the mile he runs 3:48.53 to take the record back from Ovett whose response is to run 3:48.40. Coe takes the record again by running 3:47.33.

Steve Cram wins the 1500m at the 1982 European Championships in Athens. Sebastian Coe is second in the 800m and David Moorcroft third in the 5000m. In the same year David Moorcroft sets a world record for 5000m of 13:00.41.

Also in 1982, a British team (Peter Elliott, Garry Cook, Steve Cram and Seb Coe) set a new world record for the 4 × 800m relay of 7:03.89.

In 1983, Steve Ovett's record for the 1500m is broken by former South African runner, Sydney Maree. Ovett regains the record by running 3:30.77.

Helsinki plays host in 1983 to the first World Championships. Steve Cram wins the 1500m and Colin Reitz takes the bronze in the 3000m steeplechase.

At the 1984 Olympic Games in Los Angeles, Sebastian Coe repeats his 1980 placings with gold in the 1500m and silver in the 800m. Steve Cram takes the silver medal in the 1500m. Mike McLeod wins silver in the 10,000m, Charles Spedding bronze in the marathon and Wendy Sly silver in the 3000m.

Steve Cram's year for world records is 1985 when he takes the 1500m from Steve Ovett by running 3:29.67 and the mile from Sebastian Coe by running 3:46.32. He also sets a new world record for 2000m of 4:51.39.

In the 800m at the 1986 European Championships in Stuttgart, British runners take all three medals in the 800m. Sebastian Coe wins from Tom McKean with Steve Cram third. Steve Cram wins the 1500m with Sebastian Coe taking the silver medal. Jack Buckner wins the 5000m and Tim Hutchings is third. Yvonne Murray is third in the women's 3000m.

At the second World Championships held in Rome, 1987, Peter Elliott wins a silver medal in the 800m and Jack Buckner a bronze in the 5000m.

In Seoul at the 1988 Olympics, Peter Elliott, despite a groin injury, wins a silver medal at 1500m and Mark Rowland takes the bronze in the steeplechase. Yvonne Murray places third in the 5000m and Liz McColgan second in the 10,000m.

1990-1999

Tom McKean (800m) and Yvonne Murray (3000m) win titles at the 1990 European Championships in Split. There are silver medals for David Sharpe (800m), Gary Staines (5000m), and Mark Rowland (3000m steeplechase).

At the third World Championships, Tokyo 1991, Liz McColgan wins the 10,000m.

Landmarks in Coaching

The success of Britain's endurance runners has been founded on tradition and good preparation. British coaches have followed closely the training methods used by the best runners of the day. These observations have been coupled with a growing understanding of the physiology of exercise to produce today's highly organised approach to the preparation of runners. Detailed here are some of the coaches who have influenced our present approach to training.

LAURI PIKHALA

During the 1920's and 30's, Finnish runners experienced outstanding success in the long distance track events. These included Paavo Nurmi who won nine Olympic gold medals and set numerous world records. He, with his Finnish coach Lauri Pikhala, developed a training system which was divided into shorter periods of work and rest. This system is thought to have been a forerunner of interval training.

WOLDEMAR GERSCHLER & HERBERT REINDELL

German athlete Rudolf Harbig brought the work of coach Woldemar Gerschler to the fore in the late 1930's. Gerschler, together with physiologist Herbert Reindell, developed a scientific approach to interval training. They used relatively short distances, 100m and 200m, 3 and 6 secs respectively slower than the athlete's best time for that distance, and saw the recovery period or interval as the strong stimulus to adaptation. It is for this reason that "Interval Training" is so named. The recovery period, which was identified as being about 90 secs, was the time the heart took to drop from 180 bpm to 120 bpm. At a later date they recommended the inclusion of longer intervals of 600m, 15 secs slower than the athlete's best for the distance.

GOSTA HOLMER

Around the same time as Gerschler, the Swedish national coach, Gosta Holmer, introduced the concept of fartlek training. This type of training was less formal than interval training and was well suited to the Scandinavian environment. It involved continuous runs through the woods, where the runners alternated periods of hard running with periods of light running. The success of Gunder Hagg and Arne Andersson was attributed to fartlek training.

EMIL ZATOPEK

Emil Zatopek's long distance running success in the early 1950's was based on a mixture of long distance running and the interval system. A typical session would have been 5-10 × 200m, 10-20 × 400m, 5-10 × 200m, all with 200m jog recoveries. This type of work was similar to that recommended by Gerschler and it developed aerobic endurance. He must also be given credit for his continuous search for new approaches to training. For example, on one occasion, when pursuing a theory that running whilst holding his breath in training would enhance his competitive performance, he was found unconscious at the side of the road. He had been trying to beat his own record for the number of telegraph poles he could pass.

MIHLOV IGLOI

Around the same time as Zatopek, the Hungarian coach Mihlov Igloi's methods were producing success with 1500m runners and steeplechasers such as Sandor Iharos, Laszlo Tabori and Sandor Rozsnyi. Igloi's training, which took place twice per day, was entirely based on interval running, but differed from that of Gerschler and Zatopek by including training at faster speeds to develop lactic acid tolerance. Between them, athletes he coached set over 30 world records indoors and outdoors.

FRANZ STAMPFL

Franz Stampfl is another famous coach who, in the 1950's, was advocating interval training. This was employed 3-4 times per week using varying distances of 400m to 1½ miles. The runs were relatively slow in the autumn, progressing in speed through the year. Stampfl was coach to athletes such as Roger Bannister, Chris Chataway and Chris Brasher.

ERNEST VAN AAKEN

The coach/doctor, Ernest Van Aaken, had been recommending an approach to training based on long slow distance running, the ethos of this system being "run long, run slow, run steady". He is said to have been committed to this approach as far back as the 1920's. However, it was in the 1960's that he had success with Harold Norpoth who broke the world record for the 2000m. Although this training might at first seem better suited to long distance runners, it was incorporated into the programmes of other successful coaches.

PERCY CERUTTY

In the late 1950's and early 60's, the Australian runner Herb Elliott came to the fore. Elliott was coached by Percy Cerutty who was associated with some very tough training regimes including sand dune running. His system involved running about 10 miles every day, with a long run of up to 35 miles once per week. He also included sand dune running, weight training and near vegetarian diet.

ARTHUR LYDIARD

The New Zealand coach, Arthur Lydiard, whose successes included Peter Snell, brought another unique approach to preparation in the early 60's. This involved a period of long slow distance running or, as he called it, marathon training. This was followed by a period of hill running for about six weeks. Then came a period of track training for about six weeks, and finally a tapering down period leading to the major race of the season. Lydiard's marathon running period extended back as far as possible and would have been built up to 100 miles per week.

British Coaching

In more recent years British coaches have made a significant impact on endurance coaching. Included here would be coaches of the stature of Denis Watts, Harry Wilson, Frank Horwill, Peter Coe, Tommy Boyle, George Gandy and John Anderson, to name but a few. Whilst other countries have developed coaching systems, British coaching enjoys the healthy position where coaches are free to interpret training principles and coaching practice to meet the individual athlete's needs. This approach has produced coaches who coach with flair and who are not slaves to a system.

RECOMMENDED READING

Mobility Training, N. Brook, BAAB, 1990.

Strength Training, M. Jones, BAAB, 1990.

Training Theory, F.W. Dick, BAAB, 1991.

Training Distance Runners, D.E. Martin and P.N. Coe, Leisure Press, 1991.

Running My Way, H. Wilson, Sackville Books, 1988.

Improve Your Running Skills, S. Peach (Ed), Usborne Publishing, 1988.

Training for Sport and Activity (3rd edition), J.H. Wilmore and D.L. Costill, W.C. Brown, 1988.

Athletic Ability & the Anatomy of Motion, R. Wirhed, Wolfe Medical Publications Ltd., 1984.

Focus on Middle Distance Running, J. Humphreys and R. Holman, A. and C. Black, 1985.

Focus on the Marathon, J. Humphreys and R. Holman, A. and C. Black, 1985.

LIST OF FIGURES

*Photograph   **Photosequence

*Photograph   **Photosequence

LIST OF TABLES